MACHINE LEARNING FOR BEGINNERS

A Math Guide to Mastering Deep Learning and Business Application. Understand How Artificial Intelligence, Data Science, and Neural Networks Work Through Real Examples

Samuel Hack

Copyright © 2019 by Samuel Hack - All rights reserved

The book is only for personal use. No part of this publication may be reproduced, distributed, or transmitted in any form or by any means, including photocopying, recording, or other electronic or mechanical methods, without the prior written permission of the publisher, except in the case of brief quotations embodied in critical reviews and certain other noncommercial uses permitted by copyright law.

TABLE OF CONTENTS

INTRODUCTION 7

THE PURPOSE OF THIS BOOK 11

WHAT IS ARTIFICIAL INTELLIGENCE? 19

HOW IS MACHINE LEARNING USED? 33

RECENT ADVANCEMENTS IN DATA ANALYSIS 45

INTRODUCTION TO STATISTICS 75

CHOOSING THE RIGHT KIND OF MODEL FOR MACHINE LEARNING 91

SUPERVISED LEARNING 97

CLASSIFICATIONS 129

UNSUPERVISED LEARNING 143

NEURAL NETWORKS 155

REINFORCEMENT LEARNING 167

ENSEMBLE MODELING 173

THINGS YOU MUST KNOW FOR MACHINE LEARNING ... 179

PROGRAMMING TOOLS 193

DEVELOPING MODELS 201

AFTERWORD 212

Introduction

Congratulations on purchasing *Machine Learning for Beginners,* and thank you for doing so.

There are many opportunities opening up in the field of machine learning. It's being adopted as a tool by almost every major industry. Whether you are interested in health care, business and finance, agriculture, clean energy, and many others, there is someone utilizing the power of machine learning to make their job easier.

Unfortunately for these industries, but fortunate for you is that there is a major shortage of talent in the field of data science and artificial intelligence. While entry-level data science jobs remain competitive, there is a major shortage of experienced data professionals who can fill the high-level roles. It's a newer field in computer science, with a younger group of individuals who make up for much of the field.

It can be very financially rewarding if you manage to land a job in data science. In 2016 the average data scientist made about $111,000, with predicted growth over the next five years. About half of data scientists working in the field have a Ph.D. It's not a requirement, but it's something to consider if you are looking into starting a real career as a data scientist.

If you are looking to add machine learning to your wheelhouse, so that you can have a better understanding of it and implement it in your own business or projects down the road, then a Ph.D. may not be necessary. But for those looking to enter the field, higher education is recommended as it will help you stand out amongst the field.

Indeed.com called machine learning the best career in 2019, and it's easy to see why. With a huge demand for talented data scientists and a lucrative payout, it's worth a look. And big data doesn't seem to be going away anytime soon with an increase in connectivity and higher than ever internet usage by both consumers and companies alike. Data is a part of our modern world, and as the complexity and size of data increases, it will take even more specialized knowledge and skills to be able to complete the task at hand.

To supplement the knowledge in this book, I highly recommend seeking further knowledge in statistics and programming. A good base of statistical knowledge is required to perform any work in machine learning because statistical mathematics provides the structure and justification for all the models and algorithms that data scientists use for machine-learning.

THE PURPOSE OF THIS BOOK

This book is not meant to be a comprehensive textbook on machine learning. Instead, it will give you a base of knowledge to continue with your study of machine learning and artificial intelligence. In order to continue your studies and master the subject, there is a large degree of studying that must be done. Will discuss the general structure and organization of machine learning models, the common terms, and the basic statistical concepts necessary to use and understand machine learning.

It's necessary to have a solid understanding of statistics and quantitative analysis to be a data scientist. After all, artificial intelligence and machine learning are rooted in statistics. This provides the anchor and foundation for the kind of mathematics needed.

While coding is not required to understand this book, it is a major component of machine learning. In order to handle large volumes of data, data scientists need to have a working knowledge of computer programming to 'tell' the data what they want it to do. This book will not offer much in the way of coding information, but it will present resources and avenues to get you started in studying coding on your own. By the end of the book, I will at least assist you in setting up Python with the necessary libraries and toolkits to help you start learning to code.

The most common language used in machine learning is Python. It's a versatile language that is relatively easy to learn and freely available. There are Python packages designed for data analysis to make your coding go faster. C++ is also quite common but more difficult to master. A third option is R, which is quite popular because it is free and open source. Students often use it because of its availability and simplicity. The drawback of using R is that it can't handle massive datasets often used in machine learning and artificial intelligence, which is somewhat limiting.

Computers in machine learning distinguish themselves by being able to not only memorize new information but apply that information to new situations in the future. There is a difference between memorizing and learning. There is an important distinction between giving a computer a line of code and creating a machine learning model.

The basic characteristic of machine learning is the use of artificial inductive reasoning. Artificial inductive reasoning means that a specific event gives you cause to generalize a characteristic. This apple is green; therefore, all apples must be green. But here you can see why inductive reasoning on its own is not always perfect, and why it's difficult to train computers to have the same thought process. One given piece of data is not necessarily representative of thousands of other possible pieces of data. Therefore, when we are using statistics and machine learning, we must be using enough data to be able to reason with confidence, without making the wrong inference based on data that is misinterpreted and becomes misleading.

There are things we do every day as humans that we think of as 'common sense.' These types of intuitive decisions cannot be explicitly programmed in a computer, because the variables that help us make our decisions are too difficult to measure. We probably don't need to see a thousand different combinations of chess pieces on a chessboard to think ahead and plan when we are given a situation we haven't seen before. We, as humans, require much fewer data to be able to infer and learn.

This is where machine learning comes in. These situations where the variables are complex, and directions can't be explicitly stated have to be learned instead. Back to the example of a computer that can play checkers. It would take way too long to teach someone to play checkers by giving them every possible move and every possible countermove. Instead, you teach someone the basics, and by playing the person learns what helps them win and what doesn't.

In the same way, it would be impossible to tell your computer every possible situation in a checkers game, and then tell the computer what it needs to do in each situation. There are far too many possibilities. Instead, you must give the computer enough data so that even when it is met with a new situation, it can respond accordingly.

Another example we will talk about later in this book uses artificial neural networks to sort whether a photo is a picture of a cat or a dog. As humans, this type of classification would be too easy. We know what a dog looks like because we have seen dogs, and we know what a cat looks like because we have seen cats.

But there is no way to explicitly tell a computer how it can tell the difference between a cat and a dog. Instead, you give the computer a set of training data with pictures of cats and dogs, and you tell the computer which pictures are of cats, and which pictures are of dogs. Eventually, the model should be able to tell you whether new, unseen pictures have a feline or a canine in them.

The problem with explicitly programmed instructions is their inability to change. If I tell a computer exactly what to do, using a programming language with explicit instructions, then the program will do a very good job of performing that task, but only that task. It won't change when it gets new information, and it won't alter its method if it performs incorrectly

Over time, a machine learning model will be able to change itself as the data changes so that it continues to adapt and remain accurate in a changing environment without guidance. This offers a huge advantage because it makes our models more adaptable to change, which is constantly around us. Without machine learning and artificial intelligence, our computers wouldn't have a way to keep up.

WHAT IS ARTIFICIAL INTELLIGENCE?

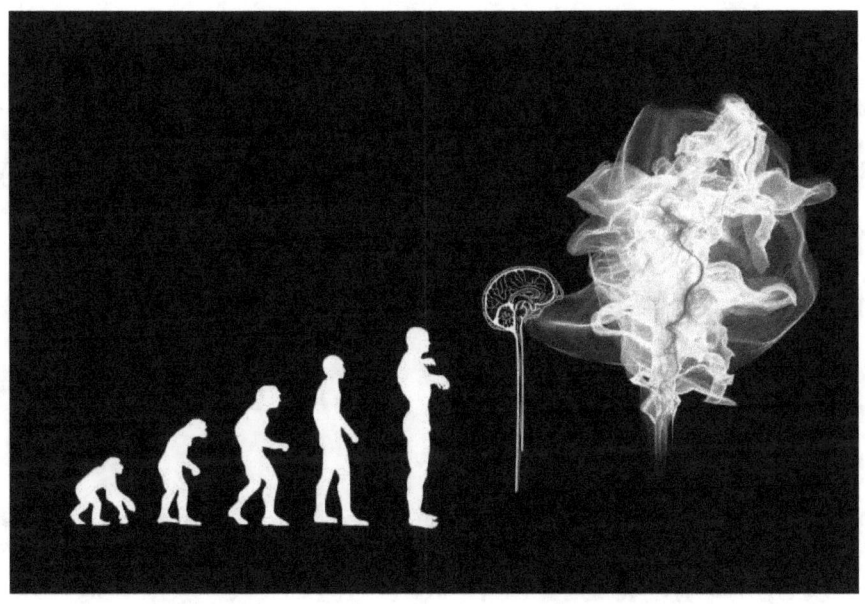

In the 1950s, separate researchers began developing the first artificial intelligence machines. Before then, only minor experimenting had been done in artificial intelligence; particularly in code-breaking during the second world war. It was an emerging field, and only some people seemed to be aware of the potential in the beginning

Now, artificial intelligence is used in a variety of applications in multiple sectors involving problem-solving, learning, planning, reasoning, and logic. It enables computers to perform tasks which normally require human thinking to perform. To 'think' like a human, computers require data from which they can learn.

Artificial intelligence holds an almost mythical place in people's minds. I bet if you said the words artificial intelligence to most people, there would be images of robots walking around acting like humans. This kind of science-fictionalization of artificial intelligence makes people wary when they hear the term. But, it's not as scary as it sounds. It has done a lot of good in medicine and business, transportation and communication. Although there have been impressive strides in the field, the misconception of a sentient computer is still a long way off. Still, the advent of self-driving cars and computers and phones that can talk stirs the imagination.

Although it sounds more like something from science fiction, artificial intelligence is in so much of our daily lives now. If it sounded spooky to you at first, let me remind you of all the technology that artificial intelligence has brought into our lives in recent years.

Last time you turned on Netflix, you were browsing a list that took the shows you watched and the movies you re-watched. It turned that list into data and created another list of recommendations. Movies it predicted that you would enjoy based on what you've already enjoyed. This is done by machine learning, a subset of artificial intelligence.

If you have a smartphone, you may use voice commands to search for things hands-free. You tell your phone that you're looking for cafes in your area and your phone says, 'searching for cafes in your area.' In a matter of seconds, a list of results appears, and you didn't even need to type anything. It recognized your voice and understood what you said. This is a part of natural language processing, another subset of machine learning. Every time you open your email account and you label spam; your email host is learning how to do a better job identifying spam. This is another type of machine learning.

So, artificial intelligence is not necessarily sentient robots who want to take over like as we know it. As of now, it's much more benign than that. It's also extremely helpful, and it's capable of learning things that we can't explicitly program it to do.

Artificial intelligence requires something called artificial reasoning, otherwise known as machine reasoning. When humans learn new things and draw conclusions, we go through a process known as inductive reasoning. We take pieces of information to draw new conclusions. Usually, there is no set rule that we are taught to go by. We learn from experience and draw our own rules by cumulative experience. For example, I could tell you that it snowed 15 times last December. Therefore, it will snow this December again. Every day in January was cold, so every day this January will be cold. So, I should bring a jacket.

We weren't born hard-wired to know that there would be snow every December, or that January is cold. We learned these things through experience and used inductive reasoning to generalize about future December's and January's. Based on our inductive reasoning, we make the logical decision to prepare ourselves and take a coat with us next winter.

The experiences we had where we say snow in December, and we were cold in January represent our 'data'. These are the inputs from our environment that we are constantly learning from.

Humans think differently from machines because we don't interpret numerical data patterns. We learn from positive and negative rewards and from the feelings we experience in our daily lives. Getting a computer to use inductive reasoning will get us closer to having 'human-like' machines

So, for computers to learn, they need to have data to learn from. Data usually needs to be numerical, so that it can be interpreted by mathematical models and algorithms. If we give a computer enough data, it will create the parameters to design its own model or algorithm, to predict new situations based on prior experience. This is the basis of machine learning. Feed the computer experience so that it can predict new outcomes in the future through inductive reasoning.

Artificial intelligence is especially interesting because computers are already better than humans at some tasks. They can draw mathematical conclusions on a dataset with thousands of inputs in a matter of seconds. No human on earth could process that kind of information so quickly. If we could use machine learning to examine data from a complex dataset that had 100 variables, we could probably learn about trends and patterns that were very complex and hard to distinguish manually. This is what makes computers such a useful tool, and why they have helped to make huge strides in data science. Using computers for data analysis makes it easier to find patterns and similarities that you don't even know exist, or that may have not even considered.

In other tasks, computers perform very poorly. Some of these tasks would seem very simple to us. Like identifying the difference between a picture of a cat and a picture of a dog. But for a computer, this is extremely complicated to figure out. Therein lies the current challenge with artificial intelligence. Bridging that gap between the type of inductive reasoning humans are capable of, and the type of reasoning computers are good at.

Key term: Inductive reasoning. Drawing on information from experiences and our environment to draw generalizations.

The ability to see the difference between these pictures based on our knowledge of cats and dogs; this is what we know as reasoning. The goal of artificial intelligence is to teach computers how to have similar abilities to human-like reasoning

Computers models have been utilized to process Natural languages. Natural language processing gives computers the ability to understand 'natural' languages, or what we know as our human languages. Natural language processing relies on machine learning techniques to understand speech and text and respond to commands and interactions.

This technology is becoming very common and accessible. GPUs (graphics processing units) are becoming more widely available and less expensive, which means data sets are getting bigger, and the use of machine learning is expanding. You may have used it when you talk to Siri on your iPhone. When you say something to Siri, your phone receives the audio. To interpret it, it turns your audio into text. Then your phone analyzes the text to derive meaning from the command that you gave it.

Natural language processing is one of the most common applications of machine learning, and we use it every day. When we use a search function on the internet, we are using natural language processing. Translation apps must take our voice or our text and analyze the sentence structure to make meaning. When you type up a paper or a word document, your word processor uses natural language processing to sift for grammatical errors and spelling mistakes.

Despite its popularity, it's a very complex field of computer science and artificial intelligence. Being able to interpret the meaning of the alphabet arranged in a virtually infinite amount of combinations requires huge amounts of data for the computer to understand what you are writing or saying.

In addition to being able to understand what we say and write; computers can also make strategic decisions based on what they've learned from data in the 1990s.

IBM created a computer called Deep Blue that defeated a world master at chess. It was the first computer to be able to perform such a task. Because of the simplicity of the rules in chess, computer scientists at IBM chose to train their computer to play. But there are thousands of potential moves and arrangements that the pieces can take once the game has started. The computer had to learn this using data.

What makes machine learning unique to other types of computer science is the ability of models to change their methods over time to suit new data. What separates a machine learning model from a regular line of explicit code is that machine learning will take in new data and improve itself. It can also perform tasks which require planning and contain strategic components. The Deep Blue computer had to be adept at analyzing possible sequences of moves, rather than just one move at a time.

The same technologies that enabled a computer to beat a world chess champion are now making it possible for self-driving vehicles to get a passenger safely from point A to point B. Compared to the relative simplicity of chess, self-driving cars must plan and interpret hundreds of variables to keep its passenger safe. It goes beyond the two-dimensional data analysis employed by machines playing chess. Self-driving cars must master multidimensional data analyses to navigate the everchanging environment on the road.

The machine learns through trial and error, repeating the task over and over and learning from failures and successes. These experiences are introduced as data, and over time, the machine will know its probability of failure or success for every possible move.

Machine learning models interpret potential states in the environment. For an algorithm that plays chess, this is all its possible moves and all its competitor's possible moves. The algorithm is an amalgamation of goals and potential actions. By using this data, it creates a plan to optimize the likelihood of achieving the goals. It also enables computers to do self-learning without specific directions through programming.

Trying to get a computer to do all these things sounds simpler in theory than it is in practice. Most of the functions we've just mentioned; from checkers to self-driving cars require advanced statistical techniques to optimize the outcome and train a machine that knows how to 'win' with a high level of accuracy.

Machine learning falls under the larger umbrella of artificial intelligence. Artificial intelligence is a branch of computer science that includes reasoning, natural language processing, planning, and machine learning. The term was first coined by a computer scientist named John McCarthy in 1956. You'll also hear the term data science, which encompasses artificial intelligence and machine learning. Data science is a broader term, but it's often used to describe machine learning. Machine learning experts are often referred to as data scientists, both in this book and beyond. There is overlap between data science and machine learning, but they are not the same thing. Data science is more of a general term, whereas machine learning is a part of data science.

HOW IS MACHINE LEARNING USED?

Machine learning is a popular buzzword nowadays. You have often heard the term machine learning thrown around, especially in data science for digital marketing. Other familiar terms like artificial intelligence, data science, and data mining may seem synonymous with machine learning. There are slight differences between these different fields, which all fall under the umbrella of data science.

Data science is the management and analysis of data, and within data science, there are many ways to analyze the data and use it to learn. Machine learning is its own field of study within the realm of computer science. The idea is to predict something, and as you add more data, compare predictions to actual outputs. Over time, your ability to predict should improve, and errors will be reduced.

One of the most important functions of the human brain is the ability to change our behavior based on the outcomes of past events and situations. If a situation has a positive outcome, we remember that, and in turn, if a situation has a negative outcome, we also store that in our memory. Later, we'll use this 'data' to make decisions about new situations. Over time, we learn how to interpret situations, even if they are totally new, and we aren't totally sure how to behave or respond.

Machine learning helps us create a mathematical way of copying the human ability to learn over time and through a new experience. Machine learning models learn over time and improve their methods of predictions, therefore improving outcome. Past data is compiled, and over time, the model can make better and more accurate predictions. Over time, the program will be able to make more accurate predictions because of the new data it's been given. It learns over time how to do a better job at completing a given task.

Some of it has inspired science fiction, spurring fears that artificial intelligence will surpass us and take over the world. Eventually, our machines will be able to do everything that we can do, but better. Our computers will surpass us and leave us behind. Despite common fears, artificial intelligence is still a relatively young field with a long way to go. While it may not take over the world anytime soon, machine learning has changed the job market today, and it will only continue to change it in the future.

Jobs that used to require human thinking can now be done with machine learning. Factories, medical diagnosis, and even taxis have the potential to be done using artificial intelligence and machine learning. Data is becoming an ever more important field of study. Patterns in data can be impossible to interpret with a human brain, which is why we use machines to detect patterns.

In finance, machine learning is being used to detect fraud. Algorithms are now capable of detecting when a financial transaction has characteristics of fraud.

Companies can spot fake reviews by recognizing word patterns and timing for review postings that are more likely to be fake.

Our phones use speech recognition to understand what we are saying and to respond to our requests. Social media uses complex data analysis to recognize patterns in our photos and can tell who is in a picture before we even begin tagging. All of this is done by the collection of data and interpretation through machine learning. The patterns in photographs that tell who appears is data which is analyzed and improved upon by machine learning models.

In 1959, Arthur Samuel first popularized the term "machine learning." A graduate of MIT, he chose to create a computer program that could play checkers. He chose checkers because of its relative simplicity, but also because checkers contains many possible strategies. This predated IBMs deep blue, but the theory was the same. Let the computer learn over time with new data.

The computer considered the positions of every checker piece, and each potential move. Each move had a score with the probability of winning. The algorithm included factors like the number of pieces on the board and the number of pieces that had been kinged.

The algorithm memorized every combination of positions that it experienced, in a process called rote learning. For each of these combinations, it remembered the score of the probability of winning. Over a few years, Samuel played countless games with the machine in order to teach it how to play.

Machine learning was coined to express what the machine was doing to learn how to beat opponents. The machine had to learn how to play checkers and learn how to reduce its errors to win. This was the first time that machine learning was talked about as its own independent field of study outside of computer science or artificial intelligence.

Sandford University refers to machine learning as "The science of getting computers to act without being explicitly programmed." Samuel's computer didn't have to be programmed to remember every possible checkers move. Instead, the 'experience' that the machine gained served as data, and it learned from each game to optimize its strategy for winning. Statistics offers the structure and mechanics for machine learning. Despite the birth of the term machine learning in 1959, it has only been recognized as a separate field of computer science first since about the 1990s with the advent of Deep Blue.

Normal computer programming uses an input command to direct the model. An example of this would be plugging 4+4 into your python window. It will give you the answer, 8. Instead, machine learning uses what's called input data. Input data is what the machine needs to learn, whereas input command would mean that the machine is not self-learning. The programmer doesn't specify what he wants the answer to be. Instead, the machine interprets the data on its own, which makes it self-learning. In machine learning, the machine takes data over time and uses it to create a new model for something.

The machine will detect patterns and structure within data, based totally in statistical logic. It is completely based on mathematical algorithms. Rather than using intuition to search for patterns, patterns our found at a quantitative and logical level by the machine learning model. The more relevant data a machine is exposed to, the better it understands and can predict the outcome of the model.

Machine learning is only useful if you can make it improve the efficiency of the task you are trying to achieve. Before you begin with your data, you need to think specifically about what you are trying to learn. What is the question you are trying to answer with your machine learning model?

The environment is always changing, and if you want to create models that are up to date and work in the changing environment, then you need to continue to teach your model with new data. If you want your data to be useful to you, then you need to find a way to keep your data up to date with the current questions.

Find out as much as you can about your market, or about the environment that you are operating in. What kind of things are you trying to understand? If you are using machine learning to improve your business, then find out what kinds of variables make up your customers choices. These are the things you want to identify and study in your models. You must have a good understanding of your subject before you can use machine learning to study it. It's impossible to predict the future, even with machine learning at your disposal. But if you can adapt your models to the ever-changing data, then you will have a better shot in the long run than if you stay stagnant.

Before you start, you should have a good amount of knowledge of the data you are choosing. Where did it come from, and how was it collected? What format is it in, and what will the challenges be while interpreting it? These are the types of questions you should be asking when you begin, and I hope that with this book, you'll be able to look critically at the data before you begin.

It's not a one-size-fits-all approach to predicting the future, and it won't give you the magic formula for anticipating future business trends or stock prices. But it is an incredibly useful tool that when used right, can make decision making much easier.

Opportunities to experiment with machine learning are growing. It's a challenge today to find the right people to fill the jobs required for the development of machine learning and artificial intelligence. It's a specialized field, and there is a short supply of people with statistical and computer science knowledge to move the field forward. This means there is an opportunity for people who possess the skills necessary for machine learning.

Recent Advancements in Data Analysis

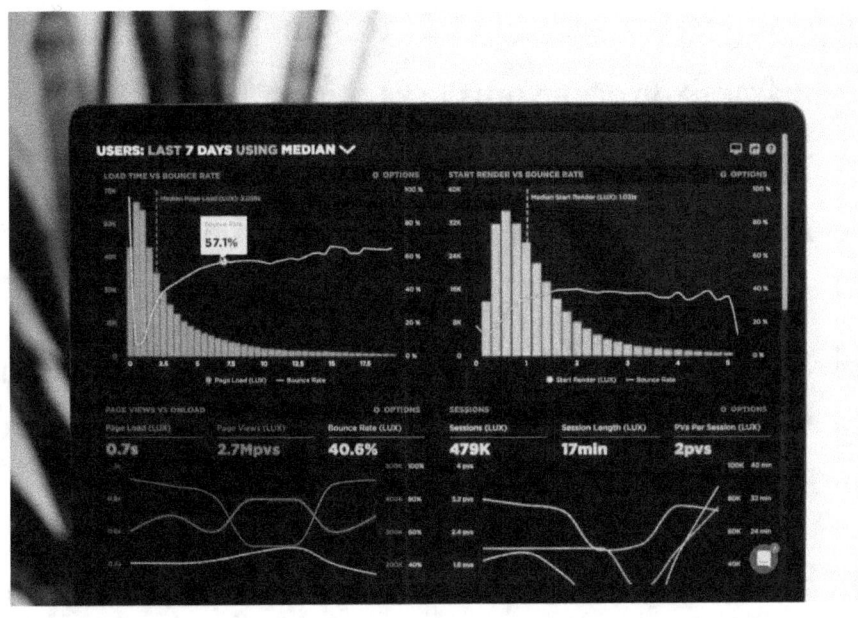

Machine learning has changed drastically since its beginning in 1959 with Arthur Samuel's checkers playing computer. But it has changed more in the last two decades than in its entire history, especially with the improvement of computing power. In the past, machine learning and big data analysis used to be very limited. Only larger companies with expensive tech had the ability to use data to make business decisions.

Now, almost anyone can utilize some amount of data for business or other purposes with a laptop or home computer. Data is much easier to come by, and the machines to process it have also become much more accessible. What used to take expensive computing power can now be done much more cheaply, and quicker.

The advent of cloud technology has made it easier for smaller businesses access to large datasets without the need for massive amounts of data storage. Now machine learning has become a completely different field of computer science, with people who specialize in machine learning and data science as its own field.

More and more things are connected nowadays, and the internet continues to grow larger and larger all the time. This means that access to data is increasing, but also the sources of data are changing. Even people's cars have computers in them, which means that when they drive, they are creating data which can be interpreted. The vast majority of Americans carry a cell phone and do internet shopping and use apps for navigation. People use their phones to control home appliances, which is another potential source of data. There are Fitbits and smartwatches which allow people to track data about their health.

The more devices, not just computers, and phones, but devices of all kinds, are connected, the greater the possibilities in terms of collecting and studying data. This connection of everything; smartphones, smart cars, etc. make people nervous that they may be at risk of losing their private data. They fear that their privacy at stake and someone is always watching them. But machine learning and data analytics are making our lives much easier. Finding the right products is easier, navigation is easier, and finding new music is easier. This is all thanks to machine learning.

Image Recognition

One of the applications of machine learning models is for the sorting and classification of data. This type of classification can even be used for the classification of images. Search engines use this kind of algorithm to identify photos, and social media sites now use face detection to identify a person in a photo before the photo is even tagged. They do this by learning from data compiled from other photos. If your social media account can recognize your face in a new photo, this is because it has created models using data from all the other photos on your account.

Image recognition techniques require deep learning models. Deep learning models are made with an artificial neural network, which will be covered more extensively later in this book. Deep learning is the most complex type of machine learning in which data is filtered through several hidden layers of nodes. They are called hidden layers because the models are unsupervised, meaning that the features identified by the model are not chosen by the data scientist beforehand. Usually, the features are patterns that the model identifies on its own. Features identified in neural networks can be quite complicated, the more complicated that the task is the more layers that the model will have. Image sorting models might only have two or three layers, while self-driving cars will have between one and two hundred hidden layers.

We have made big strides in this in recent years, because of the increased availability of computing power. Imagine the computing power that it requires to pass thousands of data points through hundreds of stacked nodes simultaneously. Deep learning and artificial neural networks have become more feasible in the last decade, with the improvement of computers and the reduction of cost to process large amounts of data. Especially with the advent of the cloud, which allows data scientists to have access to huge amounts of data without using physical storage space.

There is a website called ImageNet, which is a great resource for data scientists interested in photo classification and neural networks. ImageNet is a database of images that is publicly accessible for use in machine learning. The idea is that by making it publicly accessible, the improvement of machine learning techniques will be a cooperative effort with data scientists around the world.

ImageNet's database has around 14 million photos in its database, with more than 21,000 possible class groups. This allows a world of possibilities for data scientists to be able to access and classify photos to learn and experiment with neural networks.

Each year, ImageNet hosts a competition for data scientists worldwide to create new models for image classification. Each year the competition gets harder. Now they are starting to transition to classifying videos instead of images, which means that the complexity and level of processing power required will continue to grow exponentially. Using the millions of photographs in the database, the ImageNet competition has fostered groundbreaking strides in image recognition made during the last few years.

Modern photo classification models require methods capable of very specific classification. Even if two images should be put in the same category, they may look very different. How do you make a model that can distinguish between them?

Take, for example, these two different photos of trees. If you were creating a neural network model that classified images of trees, then ideally you would want your model to categorize both as photos of trees. A human can recognize that these are both photos of trees, but the features of the photo would make them very difficult to classify with a machine learning model.

The fewer differences the variables have, the easier they are to classify. If all your photos of trees looked like the image on the left, with the tree in full view with all its features, then the model would be easier to make. Unfortunately, this would lead to overfitting, and when the model is introduced to data with photos like the one on the right, your model wouldn't be able to classify it properly. We want our model to be capable of classifying our data, even when they aren't as easy to classify.

Incredibly, ImageNet has been able to make models capable of classifying data with many variables, and very similar data. Recently, they created Image recognition that can even identify and categorizes photos with different breeds of dog. Imagine all the variables and the similarities that the model would need to recognize in order to tell the difference between dog breeds properly.

The challenge of identifying commonalities between a class is known as Intra-class variability. When we have a picture of a tree stump and a photo of a tree silhouetted in a field, we are dealing with intra-class variability. This problem is how variables within the same class can differ from each other, making it harder for our model to predict which category they fall in to properly. Most importantly, it requires a lot of data over time to improve the model and make it accurate.

In order to have an accurate model despite high levels of intra-class variability, we will need to use additional techniques with our neural network models to find patterns among images. One method involves the use of convolutional neural networks. Rather than having just one model or algorithm, data is fed through several models which are stacked on top of each other. The neural networks convert images features into numerical values to sort them.

Unfortunately, it would be beyond the scale of this book to try and understand the way these deep neural networks operate, but there are many books available that cover those types of models and also include more comprehensive explanations of the coding required to perform these types of analysis.

Speech Recognition

Improvements in artificial intelligence have made speech recognition more useful very recently. Most of our smartphones now have some level of speech recognition ability, which involves machine learning. Speech recognition takes the audio data we give it, and it turns it into text that can be interpreted.

The difficult thing about speech recognition is the irregularities in the way that people speak. Like intra-class variability. You and I may have different accents and different inflections that are hard to account for when you are teaching a computer how to understand the human voice. If we both say the same word with different accents, how do we teach the model to understand us?

Speech recognition also uses neural networks to interpret data, like image recognition. This is because the patterns in audio data would probably not be recognizable by a human. Data scientists use sampling in order to interpret data and make accurate predictions despite the variances in peoples voices. Sampling is done by measuring the height and length of the sound waves, which believe it or not can be used to decipher what the user is saying. The recorded audio is converted into the wave map of frequencies. Those frequencies are measured by numerical values and then fed through the neural networks hidden layers to look for patterns.

Medicine and Medical Diagnosis

Machine learning is not just useful for digital marketing or making computers respond to your requests. It also has the potential to improve the field of medicine, particularly in the diagnosis of patients using data from previous patients.

With as much potential as machine learning has for medical diagnosis, it can be challenging to find patient data that is available to use for machine learning because of the laws surrounding patient privacy. Its gradually gaining acceptance in the field of medicine, which means data is becoming available to data scientists. Unfortunately, up until now, it has been difficult to have enough meaningful data to be able to make models regarding medical diagnosis. But the technology is there and available to be used.

Machine learning could use image recognition to diagnose x-rays by taking data from several patients to imaging scans in order to make predictions about new patients. Clustering and classification can be used to categorize different types of the same disease so that patients and medical professionals can have better a better understanding of the variation of the same disease between two patients, and their likelihood of survival.

Medical diagnosis with machine learning can reduce diagnosis errors made by doctors or give the doctors something to offer them a second opinion. It can also be used to predict the probability of a positive diagnosis based on patient factors and disease features. Someday, medical professionals may be able to look at data from thousands of patients about a certain disease to make a new diagnosis.

But medical diagnosis is just one of the numerous ways that machine learning could be utilized in medicine. Medical datasets remain small today, and the science of machine learning still has a lot of unmet potential in the field of medicine.

Stock Predictions

Stock traders look at many variables to decide on what to do with a stock, whether they want to buy or sell or wait it out. They look at certain characteristics of a stock, and trends in the market environment to make an educated guess on what they should do. This is the way it has been done for years. Brokers and traders had to do research manually in order to make the best guess.

Machine learning can now be used to do the same thing, except that machine learning can do it much faster and more efficiently. In order to be an effective trader, you must be able to analyze trends in real-time so that you don't miss out on opportunities. Machine learning can help traders with finding similarities between stock to make financial decisions using statistical data.

Traders can use linear regression models to study data about past trends in stock market prices, and what variables cause a stock price to go up and down. They can use these regressions to decide on what to do with a stock.

Often, traders who want to analyze the performance of stock do so by utilizing what's called a support vector machine. A support vector machine is a classification model where data points are separated by a boundary line, with one category on a side and a different category or another. Traders will use support vector machines to classify which stocks to buy and which stocks to sell. Using certain variables that should be indicative of the performance of a given stock, that stock is placed on the side of the boundary line that denotes whether the price is likely to go up or go down.

Deep learning is also commonly applied in making stock models. The hidden layers of a neural network may be useful in identifying unseen trends or characteristics of a stock that could cause them to rise or fall in price.

There is no such thing as a sure bet or a risk-free investment. This was true when people made decisions, and it's still true now when we use data science to make financial predictions. It's important to remember that investing in the stock market will always be risky. It's impossible to create a model that will predict anything reliable about the stock market.

It's wild and unpredictable. But we've already learned that machine learning can find patterns that humans may not be capable of finding on their own.

If you understand that trends in the stock market may be totally random and unpredictable, then it's useful to have another model that will help you estimate a stocks predictability. Knowing how accurate your predictions are for a given stock, is just as important as the predictions itself. Create a separate model to measure the predictability of a given stock, so you know how reliable your predictions are. Different stocks will have varying levels of predictability. It's important to illustrate that with your model so that you can choose from the most reliable predictions.

Traders will continue to make the final call on whether or not a stock will go up or down in value. But data science and machine learning can streamline the process of analyzing information that will help the decision process. Which is why you will see more and more examples of machine learning models used in predicting stock, and why you should at least make yourself familiar with the idea.

Learning Associations

Marketers in all fields, from brick and mortar retail to online retail, are always seeking ways to link products together, and increase sales. Whether you own a small bike shop or a massive online warehouse, finding patterns in your customer's buying habits will help you make proactive decisions to drive sales and make more money.

Most of us will visit a grocery store during any given week. Grocery stores are a perfect example of using product positioning to get sales. Any given grocery store will organize itself so that similar items are placed together. Baking goods have their own aisle, while fruits and vegetables have their place. They do this for two reasons; it makes it easier for the shopper to find what they need and improves the customer experience. Also, product positioning can help connect customers with products that they are willing to buy but weren't seeking when they first walked in the store.

Beyond just putting the vegetables in the same aisle, there is another strategy that grocery stores can implement to steer customers towards certain products. They might infer characteristics of a customer buying a specific product, and use that to recommend other, unrelated products. For example, you can assume that someone who buys fresh vegetables from the vegetable aisle eats healthier. You could put smoothies in the vegetable aisle, in the same refrigerator where you keep fruit. If a customer comes in looking for craft beer, you can tempt them with a snack and place the kettle chips in the same isle as 12 packs of light beer.

If all of that makes sense to you, then you are on your way to understanding a technique called collaborative filtering. It's a machine learning technique that's widely used in internet marketing. If your search data shows that you've been browsing airline tickets to Cancun, you might start to notice advertisements for swimsuits showing up on your browser.

Marketing data scientists are always trying to answer this question; how can we use data to find a way to link a product with its target market? It's about utilizing data to link two otherwise unrelated products together to drive sales.

It's a way of making recommendations to a customer based on what you know about them. Machine learning can often find similarities or buying patterns in customers that we may not have known to look for. This is a powerful marketing tool that's starting to emerge in the modern age. Before, most marketing agencies had to use intuition to find their target markets. Now, data scientists can use quantitative data to draw a more accurate picture of their ideal customer. If you're interested in using machine learning in digital marketing, then this is a topic you should be familiar with.

Collaborative filtering is different from just advertising a similar product to a customer. You are making predictions about a customer's taste or preferences based on data you've gathered from other customers. You base this prediction on a correlation that you have found between two products, and then a measure for the likelihood that the product Y will be bought with product X. You use these estimates of correlation to decide on what to market and to whom.

Spotify uses a similar process when its making song recommendations. It uses data from all the music you have liked over time. If there is a correlation between two artists, meaning that a lot of people have both artists in their library, the model can predict the probability that you will like the other artist.

The more products you have in your store, the more intensive it will be to find these correlations. In a perfect world, you will be looking for correlations between every different combination of product that you have in your store.

This method for finding the probability that you will like one product based on buying another product is called the Apiori Algorithm. There are three criteria that need to be met to affirm that there is a correlation between the two products and that you should link them somehow in your store. The first criterion is support. This gives you a measurement of the popularity of a specific product. Out of all your transactions, how often does this item appear in peoples shopping cart?

The second part is the confidence in the correlation between the two products. How likely is it that customers will buy Y product when they purchase X product? Finally, what is the lift of product Y? In other words, how likely is it that someone will buy Y with X, based on the popularity of Y alone.

The model can also use data from things like purchases, social media engagements, etc. to make a prediction on the type of product you will like. This distinguishes it as machine learning rather than just data analysis because the model was looking for similarities, but the programmer didn't ask for a specific output. Maybe there are certain features or characteristics of the group that the programmer isn't even aware of. Maybe with unsupervised machine learning, the data tells us that there is a high correlation between the two types of customers. These correlations are happening all around us with similarities between groups of people. Sometimes, it requires a good computer model to spot the patterns in the data. Machine learning can find similarities that would be impossible to see without the help of computers and good modeling.

Data scientists in marketing sectors are already using statistics to improve their stores online, and if you want to keep up with online retail then its advisable to start reading about how data can help you identify similarities and trends between products, using machine learning as your tool.

Finance

The financial industry is seeing an increase in the use of machine learning. The use of data science and machine learning models makes the decision-making process faster and more efficient for financial institutions. The possibilities and applications of machine learning can be misunderstood, which means it is often underutilized or misused in finance sectors.

Work that was once tedious and required hundreds of hours of human work can now be done by a computer in a matter of a few minutes. A common example is the use of machine learning for call center and customer service work. Many of the tasks that once required a human operator can now be done over the phone with a robot that is designed with machine learning.

In addition to customer service, banks can now process and analyzing contracts and financial information from thousands of customers that would otherwise be labor-intensive — used to create credit reports and predict the likelihood that a customer will default on a loan. Machine learning techniques can look at a history of transactions of a borrower before the bank decides on whether they should loan money to that individual.

Machine learning is also being utilized in fraud prevention. It has made the finance industry more secure. Machine learning has improved the bank's ability to detect patterns in transactions that are indicative of fraud. Rather than having people assigned to monitor the transaction and look for signs of fraud, machine learning models can learn from fraud data to find patterns by automatically sifting through millions of customer transactions.

Spam Detection

A common example of a relatively simple machine learning tool is spam detection. If we are using supervised learning, defining the variables that are relevant, then the model will have certain characteristics to look for in email messages received. The model might look for certain keywords or phrases in order to detect if an email is spam or not. Words like 'buy' or 'save' might let your inbox know when you are receiving spam email. The problem with this method is there are many cases in which those words might not necessarily mean spam. There might be other keywords or combinations of words that we would overlook.

This is where reinforcement learning comes in. There are so many characteristics that may be indicative of spam email, some of them we may not even be able to explain. Reinforcement learning will allow to model to find these patterns on its own, without explicit guidance. Instead, we tell the model when it has identified spam correctly. Sometimes we find an email message in our inbox that the model didn't classify as spam, so we move it to our spam folder manually. Now the model knows that this message is spam, and this piece of data is added to the model to improve the prediction next time. So over time, the machine improves as it gets more relevant data.

This type of machine learning is known as classification. Our output falls into discrete categories. In statistics, discrete variables are variables which can be identified in only a finite number of categories. An example of a discrete variable would be the number of cars sold by a car dealership in a week. It's discrete because the car dealership can't sell half a car. The variable must be a whole number.

Introduction to Statistics

Statistics is the mathematical science of data. It is a practice by which data is collected, observed, and analyzed in order to infer meaning and examine quantifiable relationships between different variables. Machine learning is a form of inferential statistics, meaning that by examining the relationship between variables, we should be able to come up with predictions for new variables.

Statistics is used in a wide variety of disciplines. It's used in biology to study and examines animal and plant life. It has wide applications in the business world from making stock market forecasts to analyzing consumer behavior. Economists use statistics to explain quantifiable patterns in world markets. In medicine, statistics can be used to improve the way that doctors and disease specialists look at the spread and prevention of disease.

Statistics make up the core of machine learning. If you aren't willing to dive into statistics, then machine learning isn't for you. Machine learning uses statistical algorithms to help computers learn. Machine learning is all about the tracking of data and how computers can use data to improve themselves.

There are two types of statistics which are relevant to this book. The first one is descriptive analysis, which you might use during the beginning of your modeling process to look for indicators in your data. But most of what we do in machine learning falls into a different category called predictive analysis.

Key term; Descriptive analysis. The descriptive analysis helps us examine we are right now. Looking at our current situation in context to the past and seeing why things are the way they are. Why do some things sell better than others? What trends are we seeing in products currently on the market?

Key term; Predictive analysis. Predictive analysis helps us to see and understand what will happen in the future based on indicators that are currently present. When we are using machine learning for predictive analysis, it's important for us to stay current and continue to feed the model new data. What trends should we be on the lookout for?

Machine learning is just another way to understand the data that is around us and to help us understand our present and predict the future. But it requires data from the past and present so that we can find trends and see where they might lead.

Within statistics, there are two over-arching categories of data that we will use, and all our data will fall into one category or the other somehow.

The first category is **quantitative data**. Quantitative data is data that can be measured with a numerical value. Some examples of quantitative data include height, income, or the square footage of a house. All these variables can be measured by some number, which makes them quantitative.

The second category is **qualitative data**. Qualitative data is data where the variables are assigned to categories or classes. Examples of qualitative data would include someone's gender, blood type, or whether a piece of real estate has a pool or not. This data can be sorted by its identity and is non-numerical. Therefore it is qualitative.

Quantitative data can either be discrete or continuous. If we have a data set where there is a variable recording the number of patients that a hospital had last year, this would be considered discrete. Discrete variables have a finite amount of values that they can have, and they are always whole numbers. It would be impossible to have half a patient or a percentage of a patient. Therefore this variable is discrete.

Data can also be continuous. An example of continuous data would be a variable for income. Income can take on half values, and there is a virtually infinite amount of possibilities for the value of income in data.

Some other important terms to remember are the mean, median, and mode. You will often hear these three things referred to in this book when we are talking about regressions. These are all different measures of central tendency. The mean is our average value for data. If we have a variable for a person's age, we will find the mean of age by adding all the ages together and then dividing by the number of respondents in a data set.

The **median** is the value in the middle of the dataset. If you took all the responses for age and found the response that was in the exact middle of a sorted list of responses, then this would be your median.

The **mode** is the response that occurs the most frequently. If we took a sample of eleven people's ages and found that the ages were 19, 19, 20, 21, 22, 22, 22, 23, 24, 24, 25 then the mode would be 22, because it occurs the most frequently in this sample. The median would also be 22 because it happens to be in the middle of this sorted list of responses.

When you are making a statistical model, there are many important terms that have to do with the accuracy of our models. The most important, and the most frequently mentioned in this book are bias and variance. These are different kinds of prediction errors that can occur when we are creating statistic models. Ideally, we'd like to minimize the prevalence of bias and variance in our models. They will always be present, and as a data scientist, you will have to find the right balance of bias and variance in your models, whether that's by choosing different data or using different types of models. There are many ways to reduce variance and bias within a model, dependent on what you are trying to do with the data. By trying to reduce these with the wrong approach, you run the risk of overfitting or underfitting your model. When your model is **biased**, it means that the average difference between your predictions and the actual values is very high.

Variance is how to spread out our predicted data points are. Usually, the variance is a result of overfitting to the sample data we used to create the model. It doesn't do very well at predicting the outcome of new variables.

There will always be some level of error in your models. It's a fact of life that no matter how good you are at predicting something, there is always some random or nonrandom variation in the universe that will make your prediction slightly off from the true outcome.

I've created a visual example of four bullseye targets to help illustrate the difference between models suffering from high bias and variance. In this instance, the center of the bullseye represents the true value that our model is trying to predict. The top left corner is the ideal model. Notice that all our predicted data points are falling right on the bullseye. This model is quite accurate and places our predicted data points all around the true value. This is because of low variance; a lack of 'spread out' data points, and low bias; underfitting that skews our results.

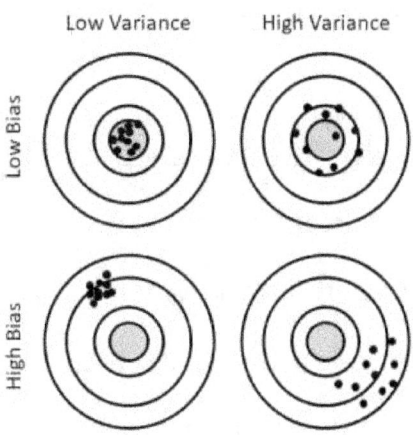

In the top right target, the model is suffering from high variance. You can see that our data points are clustered around the bullseye. Unfortunately, the average distance between the predicted values and the bullseye is high due to high variance.

In the bottom left target, the model didn't suffer much from high variance. The average distance between the predicted data points is low, but they aren't clustered around the bullseye but slightly off it as a result of high bias. This is probably the result of too little training data, which means that the model doesn't perform well when it gets introduced to new data.

The bottom right model suffers from both high variance and high bias. In this worst-case scenario, the model is very inaccurate because the average distance between predicted data points and the true value is high, and the predicted data points are skewed.

Variance can be caused by a significant degree of correlation between variables. If you use too many independent variables, this can also be a cause of the high variance. Sometimes, if the variance is too high, we can combat that by allowing a small amount of bias in the model. This is known as regularization. We'll cover that a little later.

In statistics, the **population** is the group of people or the set of data you are trying to analyze. The **sample** is the subgroup of that population, whose data you use to create your model. The **parameters** are the characteristic of the variables of the population that you are trying to identify and make predictions from in your model.

Descriptive statistics is the use of data to examine a population. Typically, descriptive statistics involve the mean or average, mode, media, size, correlation. Machine learning falls into the category of inferential statistics because we are using the data to find patterns and relations but also to make predictions based on this information. Inferential statistics, or descriptive stats, is using the characteristics of your population to make predictions. This is where your regression models and classification models will come in. When we infer something, we make a logical deduction about a population-based and the knowledge we are given.

When you are looking at data, you should also take note of the **distribution**. This is how the data is spread out on our graph. It shows the frequency of values of our data and how they appear in conjunction with one another.

We use our variance to find the standard **deviation**. Standard deviation is the average of the distances between the predicted data points and the real data points on a regression or prediction model.

We must also be sure to be aware of models that suffer from overfitting and underfitting. An overfitted model is good at predicting outcomes using the training data, but when you introduce new data, then it struggles. It's like a model that memorizes instead of learns. It can happen if you don't use random data in your training sample.

Underfitting describes a model that is too simple, and it doesn't examine any significant data patterns. It may do a good job of predicting, but the variables and parameters aren't specific enough to give us any meaningful insights if you don't have enough training data, your model could be under fitted.

One of the most commonly made mistakes when people are looking at data, is confusing correlation with causation. If I told you that every person who committed a murder last year bough eggs every week, I couldn't claim that people who buy eggs are murderers. Maybe looking at my data, I see a rise in people buying milk, as well as a rise in teen pregnancy. Would I be able to claim that there is an association between people drinking a lot of milk and teen pregnancy? Or teenagers getting pregnant caused people to buy more milk.

This is the difference between correlation and causation. Sometimes the data shows trends that seem like they are related. When two events are correlated, it means that they seem to have a relationship because they move along the graph at a similar trajectory, and during a similar space in time. Whereas causation means that the relationship between the two events involves one event causing another.

In order to imply that two things have a causal relationship, a few criteria need to be met. The first is covariation. The causal variable, and the event, it is supposed to have caused the need to be covarying, meaning that a change in one lead to a change in the other.

The second criterion that needs to be met is that the causal event needs to occur before the event it is supposed to have caused. For an event to be considered causal, it must come first.

Third, the data scientist must control for outside factors. In order to make a strong case that one thing causes another; you need to be able to present evidence that the other variables of the event are not the true cause. If the causal variable still creates the effect, even when other variables are considered, then you can claim there is a causal relationship.

CHOOSING THE RIGHT KIND OF MODEL FOR MACHINE LEARNING

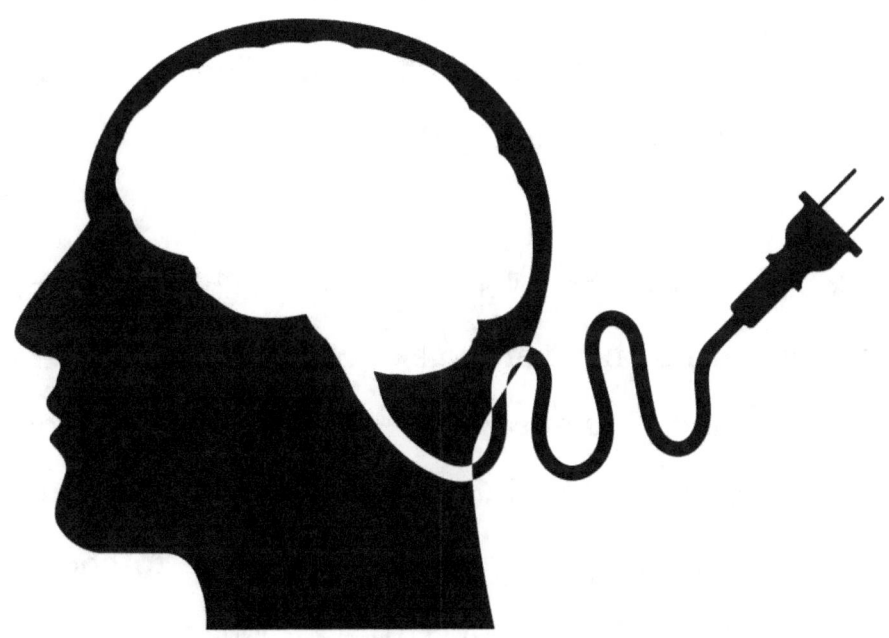

Imagine that you are a carpenter. What kind of tools do you think you will have loaded in your truck when you arrive at a worksite? You will probably have a hammer, and a drill as well as a few different types of saws. You probably have a few planes and a good set of drill bits. If you know how to do your job, then you know when you will know the purpose of each of these tools, and you will know when each one should be used. Every single one of these tools serves a specific purpose. The drill can't do a hammer's job, nor would you try to cut something with a hammer.

A data scientist who is looking to do machine learning will have his own set of tools, each serving a different purpose and designed for a different function. Depending on what kind of data you're using, and what you want to find out, you will have to choose different algorithmic models to do the job.

Statistical algorithms can serve several purposes. Some predict a value; like a regression model that predicts your income base on your years of education and work experience. Some models predict the likelihood of an event occurring, like a medical model that predicts the likelihood of a patient surviving a year, or two years, etc. Other models sort things by placing them into different categories or classes, like a photo recognition software sorting photo of different types of dogs.

Depending on the outcome you are looking for, you will need to have your statistical toolbelt. You need to familiarize yourself with the technical skills of statistics. Also, you will have to know which tool you want to use, and when to use it. Here I have created a comprehensive list of the different kinds of statistical models that are very common in machine learning. To be able to write the code to build these models on your own, I recommend that you take some time to study in the programming language that you've chosen. But this list will give you an introductory understanding of each type of model, and when they are useful.

For machine learning to be effective, you must choose the right model and the model that works best and have relevant data for the model and the question at hand.

Nowadays, especially with the use of the internet and digital marketing, there are certain questions that can't be properly understood without the use of data and machine learning that can analyze it. With machine learning and data science, you can keep track of your customers and their buying habits, so that you can better adapt to their needs when they change.

The better you are at interpreting your data, the more easily you will be able to identify trends and patterns so that you can anticipate the next change.

Machine learning can be broken down into three different categories, each one containing several unique algorithms that serve different purposes. To start, we'll talk about the differences between supervised, unsupervised, and reinforcement learning.

SUPERVISED LEARNING

In supervised learning, programmers use labeled data. Before we begin using the algorithms, the data that we are looking at is already predetermined. We know the inputs and outputs we are looking for. X, and Y. We are trying to find a relationship between X and Y that we have chosen.

After you find a relationship between X and Y, you get a model, which will predict an outcome based on those relationships that your machine has observed in the data. Supervised learning is used for regression and classification models. In machine learning, we refer to **features** as a certain measurable property or characteristic of the data.

The first type of supervised learning that we'll talk about and the first type of statistical model is called a regression. **Regression** is a model where the data input and output are continuous. There are different types of regression, but the most basic form is linear regression. We use linear regression to find a relationship between some input X and an output Y. Once we have estimated this relationship, we can predict Y with X. Linear models can, and usually do, have more than one X. In regression; output Y has a numerical value.

Regression Analysis

Regression is the simplest type of machine learning; this is usually where you start when you are first learning how to use your data. You have a set of X values, and you want to study their relationship with Y, the output. Our independent variables, the Xs in our model, are given weight, and for each value of X, it is multiplied by weight until the aggregate function creates a prediction for Y.

We can create a predictive model for Y by using data where we already know the X and Y. Regressing this information will give us the weights of X. If we have enough relevant data, eventually we will be able to predict and unknown Y with known values for X.

We graph our known Y and X values on a scatterplot, and our regression model finds the "best fit" line through the data points. The regression line is called a hyperplane. The steepness of the line is called the slope.

We can measure the distance between the predicted value and actual data point, and we call that measurement deviation. Our goal when we create a linear regression is the minimize the deviation in our predictions. The smaller that difference, the deviation is, the more accurate your model is.

Most of the statistical models used in machine learning are rooted in this first algorithm. Creating a model that will predict an outcome by plotting our data points along a line or in clusters. But the line isn't always straight, and sometimes the line doesn't show us the best fit.

An example of a regression function that is nonlinear is the Sigmoid function. The Sigmoid function creates an S-shaped curve. Instead of predicting a value, the Sigmoid function takes independent variables and produces a probability between one and zero.

Simple Linear Regression. In simple linear regression, we study the relationship between some predicted value Y and some predictor X. We call our Y the dependent variable because it is dependent on the value of X. Our X is known as the independent variable.

If you took algebra or pre-calculus in high school or college then you might remember the equation of a line was;

$$Y = mX+b$$

If you were to graph this equation, then you would have a graph that looks something like this:

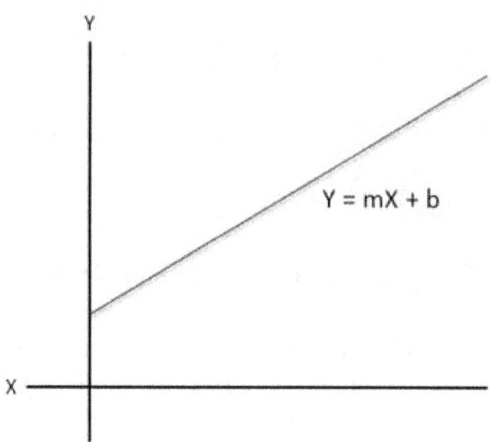

As you can see, the line shows that for every value of X there is a different value of Y. You can make a prediction for the value of Y for every new value of X. In this graph, the value of Y increases as the value of X increases. This is not always the case.

This is the most simplistic regression, but it's important to understand how it works because we will be building off it from here on out. Most of the statistical analysis involves a plot like the one pictured above, which makes some prediction for an output dependent variable based on an input, the independent variable. This is an example of supervised learning because we are specifying the Y variable and the X variable that we are using before we start modeling.

With almost all predictions, there will be more than one independent variable that will determine our dependent variable. This leads us to our next type of regression.

Multiple Linear Regression. In data science and most tasks in statistics, this will be the most popular type of regression. In multiple linear regression, we will have one output variable Y, just like before. The difference now though, is that we will have multiple Xs or independent variables that will predict our Y.

An example of using multiple linear regression to predict the price of apartments in New York City real estate. Our Y or dependent variable is the price of a New York City apartment. The price will be determined by X, our independent variables such as the square footage, distance to transportation, number of rooms. If we were to write this out as an expression it would look something like:

$$\text{apt\_price} = \beta 0 + \beta 1 \text{ sq\_foot} + \beta 2 \text{ dist\_transport} + \beta 3 \text{ num\_rooms}$$

We take sample data, data that we already have where we know our Xs and their Ys and we look at them on a graph like this:

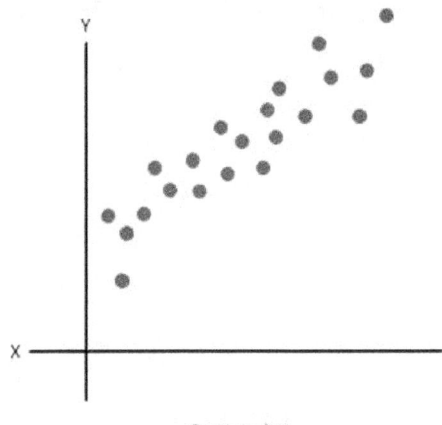

Scatter plot

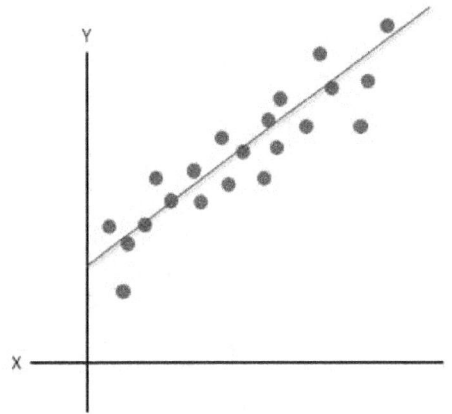

apt_price = $\beta_0 + \beta_1$ sq_foot + β_2 dist_transport + β_3 num_rooms

You can see that the values of X and Y don't create a perfect line, but there is a trend. We can use that trend to make predictions about future values of Y. So, we create a multilinear regression, and we end up with a line going through the middle of our data points. This is called the best fit line, and its how we will predict our Y when we get new X values in the future.

The difference here is that instead of writing m for slope, we have written β. This equation is pretty much the same thing as if I had written

$$Y = b + m1X1 + m2x2 + m3x3$$

Except now we have labels, and we know what our Xs and our Ys are. In the future, if you see a multilinear equation, then it will most likely be written in this form. Our β is what we call a parameter. It's like a magic number that tells us the effect that the value of our X has on the Y. Each independent variable will have a unique parameter. We find the parameters by creating a regression model. Over time, with machine learning, our model will be exposed to more and more data so that our parameter will improve, and our model will become more accurate.

We can create the model by using training data that has the actual price of New York City apartments, and the actual input variables of square footage, distance to transportation, and many rooms. Our model will 'learn' to approximate the price from real data. Afterward, when we plug in the independent variable for an apartment which has an unknown price, our model can make a prediction as to what the price will be.

This is supervised learning using a linear regression model. It's supervised because we are telling the model what answer we want it to give us; the price of New York City apartments. It learns how to predict the price more accurately, as it is given more data, and we continue to evaluate its accuracy.

Ordinary Least Squares OLS will try to find a regression line that minimizes the sum of errors squared

Polynomial Regression. Our next type of regression is called a polynomial regression. In the last two types of regression, our models created a straight line. This is because the relationship between our X and Y are linear, meaning that the effect X has on Y doesn't change as the value of X changes. In polynomial regressions, our model will result in a line that has a curve.

If we tried to use linear regression to fit a graph that has nonlinear characteristics, we would do a poor job of creating the best fit line. Take the graph on the left, for example; the scatter plot has an upward trend like before, but with a curve. In this case, a straight line doesn't work. Instead, with a polynomial regression, we will create a line with a curve to match the curve in our data, like the graph on the right

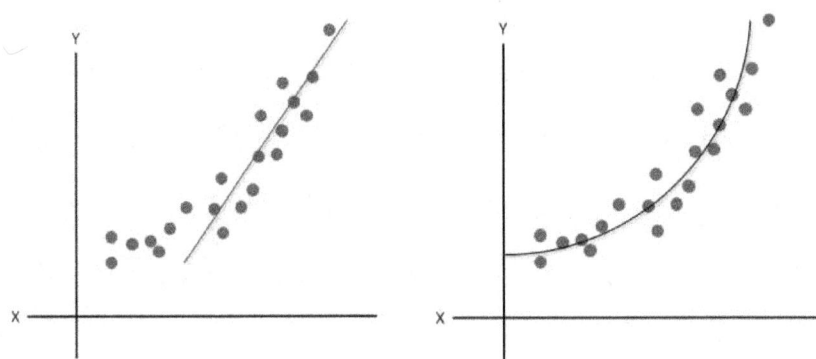

The equation of a polynomial will look like the linear equation, with the difference being that there will be some polynomial expression attached to one or more of our X values. For example:

$$Y = mX^2 + b$$

The effect that X has on Y changes exponentially as the value for X changes.

Support Vector Regression. This is another important tool for data scientists and one that you should familiarize yourself with. It is most commonly used in case classification. The idea here is to find a line through a space that separates data points into different classes. Support Vector Regression is another type of supervised learning. Its also used for regression analysis. It is a type of binary classification technique not related to probability.

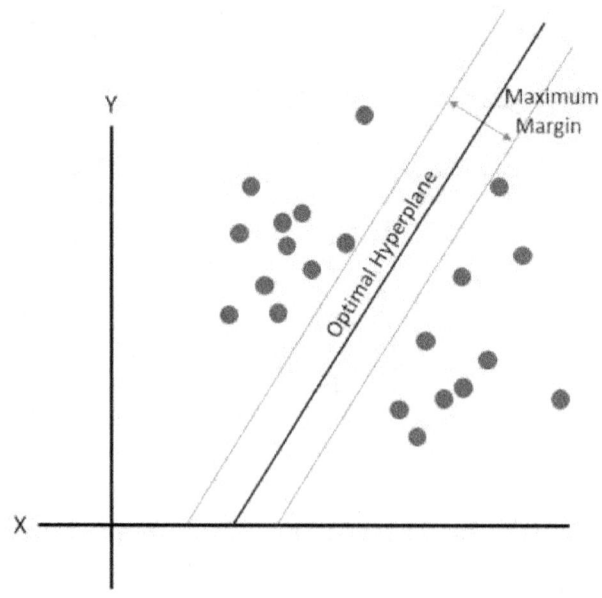

In support of Vector Regression, all your training data falls into one category or the other. You want to find out which category a new data point falls into. Your data is separated into these two classes by a hyperplane. When you're creating a model for the hyperplane, you are trying to find a hyperplane that maximizes the distance between the two classes. For example, in the next picture, you have a scatterplot where the data points can be separated into two distinct classes. In this instance, lines one and three can separate the data points into two distinct classes. However, for your model, you should choose line two because it maximizes the margin between the two classes, so they are more distinct. The wider the margin is, the better.

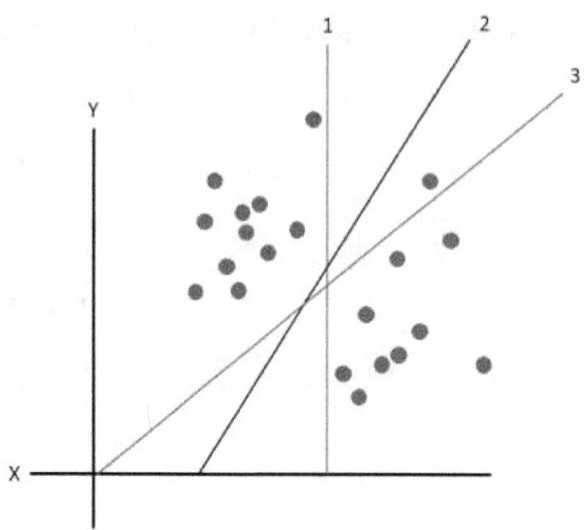

Ridge Regression. This is a technique commonly used to analyze data that suffer from multicollinearity. Using ridge regression properly can reduce standard errors and make your model more accurate, depending on the characteristics of your data.

Ridge regression can be useful when your data contains independent variables with a high correlation. If you could make a prediction about an independent variable by using another independent variable, then your model is at risk of multicollinearity. For example, if you are using variables that measure a person's height and weight; these variables are likely to create multicollinearity in the model.

Multicollinearity can affect the accuracy of your predictions. To avoid multicollinearity, be cognizant of the type of predictive variables you are using. Type of data you are using, as well as the method of collection, could be the cause of multicollinearity. There is a chance you may not have selected a broad enough range of independent variables. Your data points could be too similar because your choice of independent variables is limited.

Multicollinearity can also be caused by having a model that is too specific. You have more variables than you have data points. If you have decided to use a linear model, and that has made multicollinearity worse, then you can try to apply a ridge regression technique.

Ridge regression works by allowing a little bit of bias into the model in order to make your predictions more accurate. This technique is also known as regularization.

Another method is to improve the model's accuracy by standardizing independent variables. The simplest way is to change the coefficients of some independent variables to zero to reduce complexity. However, we won't just change them to zero, but standardization implements a system that rewards coefficients that are nearer to zero. This will cause coefficients to shrink, so the complexity of the model is less, but the independent variables remain in the model. This will give the model more bias, but it's a trade-off for more accurate predictions.

LASSO Regression. LASSO regression is another 'shrinkage' technique. A very similar approach to ridge regression in that it encourages leaner, simpler models for prediction. In lasso regression, the model is a little more stringent about reducing the value of coefficients. LASSO stands for the least absolute shrinkage and selection operator.

Data on our scatterplot is shrunk down to a more compact point, like the average of the data. Just like ridge regression, we use this when the model is suffering from multicollinearity.

ElasticNet Regression. ElasticNet regression works by combining the techniques of LASSO and ridge regression. Its main goal is to attempt to improve upon LASSO regression. It is a combination of both the methods of rewarding lower coefficients in LASSO and Ridge regression. All three of these models can be accessed in the glmnet package in R and Python.

Bayesian Regression. Bayesian regression models are helpful when we have insufficient data or data with poor distribution. These types of regressions are created using probability distributions rather than data points, which means that the graph will appear as a bell curve representing the variance with the most frequently occurring values in the middle of the curve.

In Bayesian regression, the dependent variable Y is not a value but a probability. Rather than trying to predict a value, we are trying to predict the probability of an outcome. This is known as frequentist statistics, and Bayes theorem makes up the foundation for this type of statistics. Frequentist statistics hypothesize whether something will happen, and the probability that it will happen.

When we talk about frequentist statistics, we also include conditional probability. Conditional probability involved events whose outcomes are dependent on one another. Every time you toss a coin, it is an independent event meaning that the previous coin toss does not change the likelihood of the next coin toss. Flipping a coin toss, therefore, is not a conditional probability.

Events can also be dependent, meaning that the previous event can change the probability of the next event. Say I had a bag of marbles, and I wanted to know the probability drawing different colors out of the bag. If I have a bag with 3 green marbles and 3 red marbles, and I draw a red marble, then the probability of drawing a red marble goes down on my next draw. This would be an example of conditional probability.

Decision trees

One of the models that we'll discuss later is called neural networks. They're the most advanced types of machine learning and are used for many different purposes. I've related this to decision trees because of how frequently people turn to neural networks for classification problems when there are much simpler models available. Decision trees and the related random forest models can be just as useful.

Despite the power of neural networks, they can't be used for everything. Fortunately, we have options, and the purpose of this book is to know what your options are when you decide you want to build a model. The next place to look when neural networks don't work is decision trees. Decision trees break data into subcategories using decision and leaf nodes in the shape of a tree.

Decision trees have a few advantages over neural networks (discussed later in this chapter). For one thing, neural networks require huge amounts of data and powerful computers in order to process them. The upside to using a decision tree is that they are relatively simple, especially when you compare them to neural networks. Unlike most of the models in this book, they are very easy to read a decision tree, even to the untrained eye. This makes them a good candidate when choosing a model that needs to be presented in front of stakeholders.

Decision trees are another form of supervised learning, meaning that we label the categories that we want to sort before creating the model. In some instances, decision trees can complete regression tasks, but typically they are used as classification models. When decision trees are used for regression, the leaf nodes end in probabilities.

Decision trees start with what's called a root node at the top of the tree. Then the root node is split into two nodes after the root node. Nodes are individual leaves on the tree, and the middle nodes are where the decisions are made, known as the decision nodes. The decision tree ends at the bottom in what's called a terminal node is at the bottom of a branch, where the decision is complete.

Ideally, the decision tree will sort the data quickly, layer by layer. Because of this, we call the model 'greedy' because the top nodes try to sort the data as quickly as possible so that it requires fewer layers. Like neural networks, decision trees often suffer from overfitting. A decision tree usually won't work with other sets of data because the sorting is so specific to each dataset.

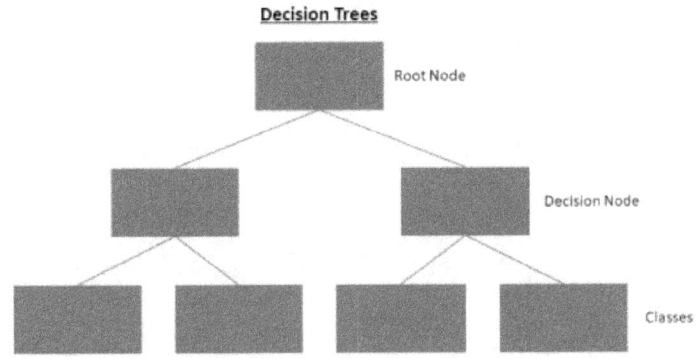

Below is an example of a decision tree about whether or not to grant a job applicant a job interview determined by qualification factors. The root node is whether or not the applicant has a college degree, followed by the decision modes which all lead to either a decision not to hire or grant an interview. You can see from this decision tree why this type of model is so specific to the specific data you are working with because every data set will have differences in qualifications and so every dataset will be sorted differently.

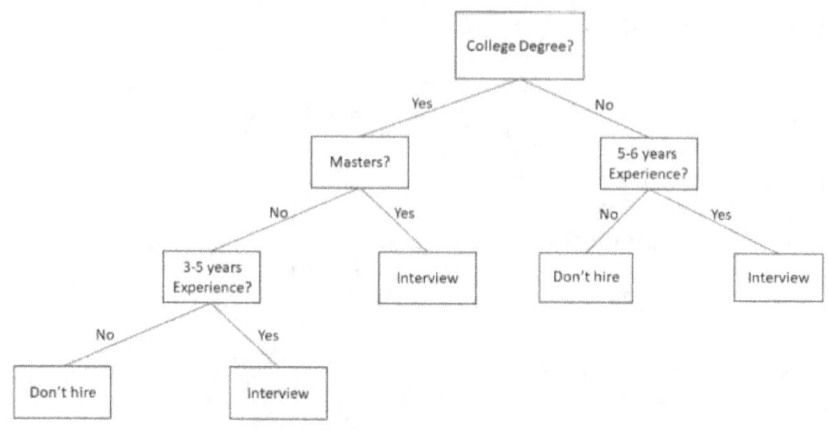

Random forests

Using just one decision tree on your model can have a limiting factor on the categories that the data is split in to, and the outcome of the decisions. Because the decision trees are 'greedy', this means that certain categories are chosen for sorting, which prohibits other categories from also being chosen. But there is an easy way to get around that. One way to diversify your decision trees and improve the accuracy of your model is by using random forests.

If a real forest is made up of several different trees, then that's exactly what a random forest is. Instead of just having one decision tree, you split the data into several decision trees. When you only have one tree, models can often suffer from high variance. Creating a random forest is a way to combat that in your model. It's one of the best tools available for data mining. A random forest is as close as you can get to a pre-packaged algorithm for data mining purposes.

In a random forest, all the trees work together. The aggregate result of all the trees is usually right, even if a few trees end up with bad predictions. To create the final prediction, the results of all the trees are tallied. Using votes from the average values of all the trees gives us a final prediction.

Because we are using data that is similar, there is a risk of correlation between the trees if they are all trying to do the same thing. If we use trees that are less correlated, then the model will perform better.

Imagine that we were to bet on a coin flip. We each have a hundred dollars, and there are three choices. I can flip the coin once, and the winner of that toss gets to keep 100$. Or, I could flip the coin ten times, and we bet ten dollars each time. The third option is to flip the coin 100 times and bet a dollar on each toss. The true expected outcome of each version of this game is the same. But if you did 100 coin tosses, you are less likely to lose all your money than if you only did a single coin toss. Data scientists call this method bootstrapping. It's the machine learner's equivalent of diversifying a stock portfolio. We want to have a model that gives us an accurate prediction. The more we split our decision trees, the more accurate our data will be. But it's important that the individual trees have a low correlation to one another. The trees in the forest need to be diverse.

How do we avoid correlation in a random forest? First, each tree takes a random sample from the dataset, so that each tree has a slightly different set of data from one another. The tree picks a feature that creates the most separation between nodes, in a greedy process, just like as individual trees. However, in a random forest, trees can only pick certain features from the overall group of features, so each tree separates by different features.

So, the trees will be uncorrelated because they are using different features to make decisions about classification. In a random forest, its best to use at least 100 trees for getting an accurate picture of the data, depending on the data set you are working with. In general, the more trees you have, the less your model will overfit. Random forest machine learning is called it a 'weakly-supervised technique' because our outcome is chosen, and we can see the sorting method, but it's up to each tree to categorize and separate variables by features.

Classification models will tell us which category something falls in to. The categories are defined by the programmer at the beginning. An example of a classification model could use a random forest would be a model that determines whether incoming emails should spam go in your 'inbox' or 'spam' folder.

To create the model, we make two categories that our Y can fall in to; spam, and not spam. We program the model to look for keywords or certain email address that may indicate spam. The presence of words like "buy" or "offer" will help the model determine whether the email message falls into the category of spam or not spam. The algorithm takes in data, and over time, it learns by comparing its predictions to the actual value of the output. Over time it makes small adjustments to its model so that the algorithm becomes more efficient over time.

CLASSIFICATIONS

A few times in this book, we've referred to classification models. While some of the models we've already mentioned are capable of classification, the following are more supervised learning models that are specifically used for classification.

Classification requires labeled data and creates non-continuous predications. In classification problems, the graphs are non-linear. There could be two classes in a classification problem, or even more. Classification models are probably the most widely used part of machine learning and data science.

The first type of classification is binary classification. With binary classification, the data is classified into two categories, denoted by 1 or 0. We call it binary classification because there are only two possible categories, and all of our data falls into one or the other.

But there are instances when we have more than two categories, and for this, we use multi-class classification models. Also, we have linear decision boundaries, where data is separated on either side of a line. Not all data can be classified into either side of a decision boundary.

The first picture has an example of a classification using a linear decision boundary. In the second image, there are almost two classes, but they are not linearly separable. In the third image, data points are mixed, and linear boundary classification is not possible. Depending on the type of data you are using, there are different model choices that will be better suited for different tasks

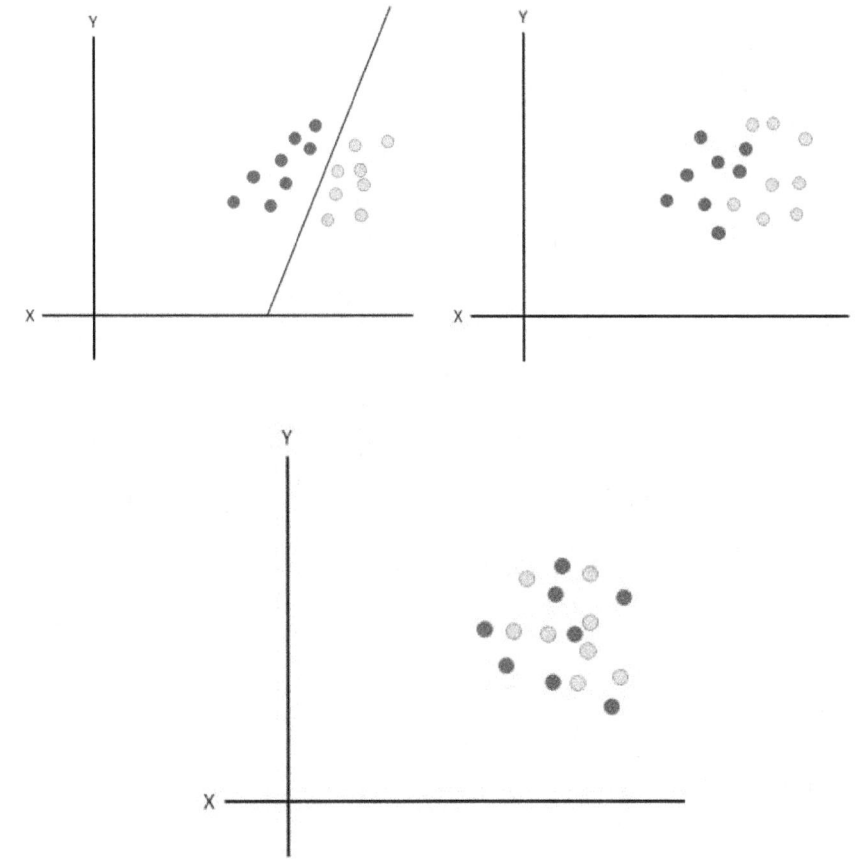

Logistic Regression/Classification

This method is used to classify dependent and categorical variables. Logistic regression calculates probabilities based on independent variables. It gives the variables the value "Yes or No" to sort them. Typically used with binary classification.

When you can't separate the data into classes by a linear boundary, like in the examples above, this is the method you must use this. It's one of the most common types of machine learning algorithms. It doesn't just sort into categories, but it also tells us the probability that a category exists.

We denote this model by taking the odds function, where p is the probability of an event;

$$\frac{p}{1-p}$$

And creating a formula called the logit

$$\log \frac{p}{1-p}$$

K Nearest Neighbors

K-nearest neighbors are one of the most straightforward and widely used methods of data classification. It's a form of supervised learning used for both classification and regression, and it's also the most basic clustering algorithm. Simply put, it's about taking a data point and putting it with the most common and nearest group on the scatterplot.

In KNN, a new data point is classified by the average median value of its neighbors K. The nearest neighbors to a new data point 'vote' for which classification it falls in to. K is the number of nearest neighbors that are voting in the model. Set k to a number- this is how many closest data points the new data point will analyze to choose which one it fits with. The closeness of data points is measured using Euclidean distance.

Take the following two images as an example. We have our data split into two classifications; the white dots and the black dots. A new data point is introduced, the triangle, and we'd like to predict which classification it falls in to.

In this model, we have chosen that K=4. If you choose k=4, then the four closest data points are analyzed. Whichever class is most prevalent amongst the neighboring data points is the class that the new data point will be placed in. In this case, you can see in the image on the right that the four white dots are the nearest classification. Therefore, the new data point is classified in that class.

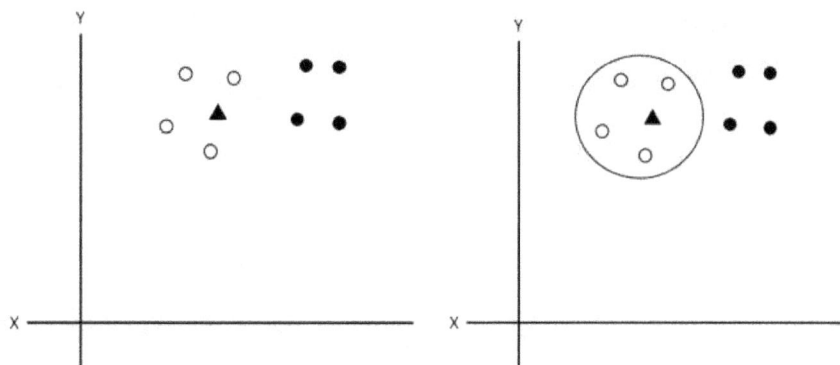

There are a few factors to consider when you are choosing the value for k. The higher the number for k is, the closer we will get to the true classification of our new data point. There is an optimal point where the value of k should stop increasing to avoid overfitting.

If you choose to use a number for K that is too low, then there is a likelihood that your model will suffer from a high level of bias. If you use a number that is too high, then the computing power required to calculate the value will be too costly. You might consider choosing to use an odd number when you choose a value for K, rather than an even number. If you use an odd number, it is less likely that you will encounter a tie between classes voting on a data point. Data scientists often choose the number 5 as a default setting for k.

If you use a large number for K, this will be very data-intensive. Large data sets are also tough to use with KNN machine learning models. If you are using larger data sets, then you must calculate the distance between hundreds or maybe thousands of data points. It also doesn't perform well when you use this method on a model that exists in more than two dimensions. Again, it has to do with the computing power required to calculate this distance between many data points.

Support Vector

Support vector is another type of classifier. It classifies using a hyperplane. Generally, we would use a support vector model with smaller datasets, where it performs quite well.

Kernel Support vector

Although we will touch on kernel support vectors, later on, they are used to sort classes that can't be separated with a linear separation line. The separation line can take on many shapes (linear, nonlinear, polynomial, radial basis, sigmoid).

Recall the classification by a linear boundary that we just talked about, where the classification looks something like the following image:

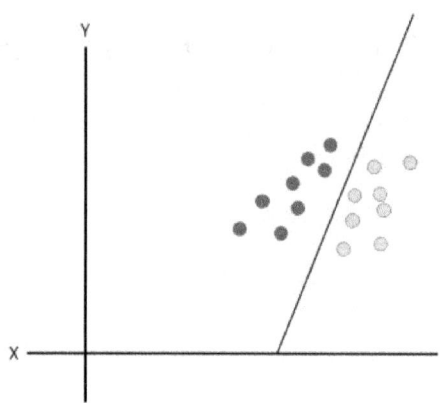

In this image, our data can be classified by a straight line that separates the two distinct categories of data. It would be convenient if data was always separable like this, but unfortunately, it's not always so neat and tidy in fact, most of the time you will have to separate the data in a way that looks more like this:

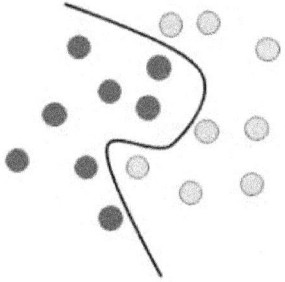

In this example, the data can't be separated by a linear boundary line. So instead we must use a technique called the kernel trick. It uses a measure of similarity between data points to classify them.

Naïve Bayes

Recall Bayes theorem from the first section on supervised learning. With Naïve Bayes models, predictors are assumed to be independent. This model is easy to use and helpful in large datasets. Its often employed to help sort spam emails.

We use Baye's rule here. The idea of Bayes Rule is that by adding new, relevant information to what we already know, we can update our knowledge based on that new information. If we wanted to know the probability of there being rain this afternoon, we could just figure out what percentage of days it rains per year. But then we found out that it rained this morning. How do you think this will affect the probability that it will rain this afternoon?

So, our ability to predict the probability of something will improve when we receive more information about the event.

Mathematically, Bayes theorem is expressed as follows:

$$P(A|B) = \frac{P(B|A)P(A)}{P(B)}$$

So, we can classify new data points using Bayes theorem. The way that works is when we are given a new data point, we calculate the probability of that data point falling into a category based on the features of that data point.

UNSUPERVISED LEARNING

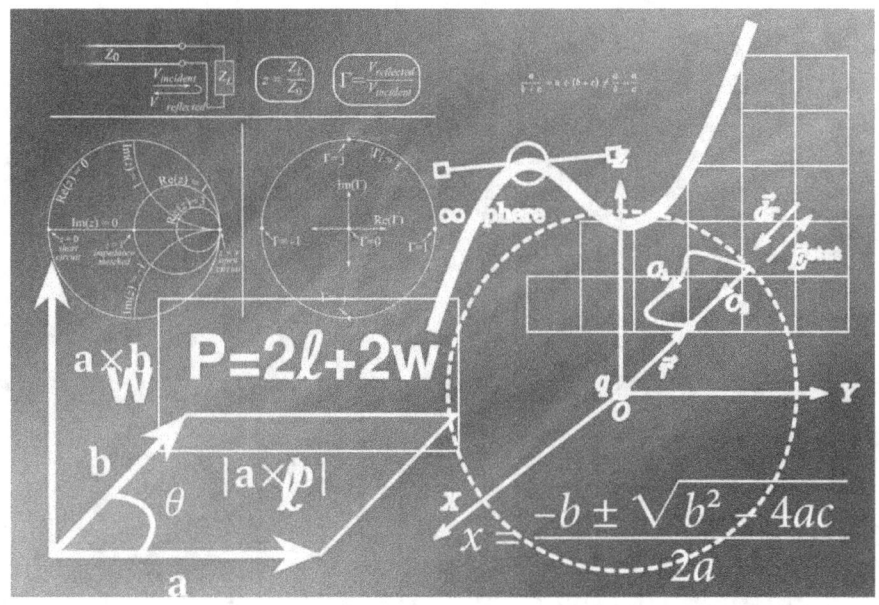

Unsupervised machine learning uses unlabeled data. Data scientists don't know the output of yet. The algorithm must discover patterns on its own, where patterns would otherwise be unknown. Find a structure in a place where the structure is otherwise unobservable. The algorithm finds data segments on its own. The model looks for patterns and structure in an otherwise unlabeled and unrecognizable mass of data. Unsupervised learning allows us to find patterns that would be unobservable without computer scientists. Sometimes massive collections of data have patterns, and it would be impossible to sift through all of it trying to find trends.

This is good for examining the purchasing habits of consumers so that you can group customers into categories based on patterns in their behavior. The model may discover that there are similarities in buying patterns between different subsets of a market, but if you didn't have your model to sift through these massive amounts of complicated data, you will never even realize the nature of these patterns. The beauty of unsupervised learning is the possibility of discovering patterns or characteristics in massive sets of data that you would not be able to identify without the help of your model.

A good example of unsupervised learning is fraud detection. Fraud can be a major problem for financial companies, and with large amounts of daily users, it can be difficult for companies to identify fraud without the help of machine learning tools. Models can learn how to spot fraud as the tactics change with technology. If you want to deal with new, unknown fraud techniques, then you will need to employ a model that can detect fraud under unique circumstances.

In the case of detecting fraud, it's better to have more data. Fraud detection services must use a range of machine learning models to be able to combat fraud effectively. Using both supervised and unsupervised models. It's estimated that there will be about $32 billion in fraudulent credit card activity next year, in

Models for fraud detection classify the output (credit card transactions) as legitimate or fraudulent.

They can classify based on a feature like time of day or location of the purchase. If a merchant usually makes sales around $20, and suddenly has a sale for $8000 from a strange location, then the model will most likely classify this transaction as fraudulent.

The challenge of using machine learning for fraud detection is the fact that most transactions are not fraudulent. If there was even a significant amount of fraudulent transactions among non-fraudulent, then credit cards would not be a viable industry. The percentage of fraudulent card transactions is so small that it can create models that are skewed that way. The $8000 purchase from a strange location is suspicious, but it is more likely to be the result of a traveling cardholder than fraudulent activity. Unsupervised learning makes it easier to identify suspicious buying patterns like strange shipping locations and random jumps in user reviews.

Clustering

Clustering is a sub-group of unsupervised learning. Clustering is the task of grouping similar things together When we use clustering, we can identify characteristics and sort our data based on these characteristics. If we are using machine learning for marketing, clustering can help us identify similarities in groups of customers of potential clients. Unsupervised learning can help us sort customers into categories that we might not have created with the help of machine learning. It can also help you sort your data when you are working with a large number of variables.

K-Means clustering

K-means clustering works similarly to K-nearest neighbors You pick a number for k to decide how many groups you want to see. You continue to cluster and repeat until clusters are more clearly classified.

Your data is grouped around centroids, which are the points on your graph that you have chosen where you want to see your data clustered. You choose them at random, and you have k of them. Once you introduce your data to the model, data points are placed in categories indicated by the closest centroid, which is measured by Euclidean distance. Then you take the average value of the data points surrounding each centroid. Keep repeating this process until your results stay the same, and you have consistent clusters. Each data point is only assigned to one cluster.

You repeat this process by finding the average values for x and y within each cluster. This will help you extrapolate the average value of the data points in each cluster. K-means clustering can help you identify previously unknown or overlooked patterns in the data.

Choose the value for k that is optimal for the number of categories you want to create. Ideally, you should have more than 3. However, the advantage associated with adding more clusters diminishes that higher the number of clusters you have. The higher the value for k that you choose, the smaller and more specific the clusters are. You wouldn't want to use a value for k that is the same as the number of data points because each data point would end up in its own cluster.

You will have to know your dataset well and use your intuition to guess how many clusters are appropriate, and what sort of differences that will be present.

However, our intuition and knowledge of the data are less helpful once we have more than just a few potential groups.

Dimensionality Reduction

When you are using dimensionality reduction, you are trimming down data to remove unwanted features. Simply put, you're scaling down the number of variables in a dataset.

When we have a lot of variables in our model, then we run the risk of having dimensionality problems. Dimensionality problems are problems that are unique to models with large datasets and can affect prediction accuracy. When we have many variables, we need larger populations and sample populations in order to create our model. With that many variables, it's hard to have enough data to have many possible combinations to create a well-fitting model.

If we use too many variables, then we can also encounter overfitting. Overfitting is the main problem which would cause a data scientist to consider dimensionality reduction.

We must choose data that we don't need, or that is irrelevant. If we have a model predicting someone's income, do we need a variable that tells us what their favorite color is? Probably not. We can drop it out of our dataset. Usually, it's not that easy to tell when a variable should be dropped. There are some tools we can use to determine which variables aren't as important.

Principle Component Analysis is a method of dimensionality reduction. We take the old set of variables and convert them into a newer set somehow. The new sets we've created are called principal components. There is a tradeoff between reducing the number of variables while maintaining the accuracy of your model.

We can also standardize the values of our variables. Make sure they are all valued in the same relative scale so that you don't inflate the importance of a variable. For example, if we have variables measured as a probability between 0 and 1 vs. variables that are measured by whole numbers above 100.

Linear Discriminant is another method of dimensionality reduction where we combine features or variables, rather than get rid of them altogether.

Kernel Principal Component is the third method for dimensionality reduction. Here, variables are placed in a new set. This model will be non-linear, and it will give us even better insight into the true parameters than original data.

NEURAL NETWORKS

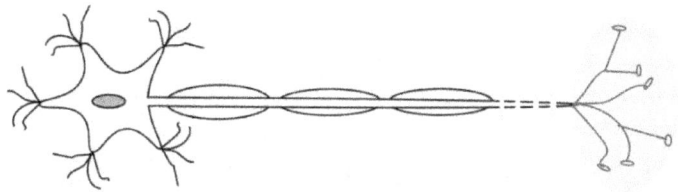

Neural networks are a form of machine learning that is referred to as deep learning. It's probably the most advanced method of machine learning, and truly understanding how it works might require a Ph.D. You could write an entire book on machine learnings most technical type of model.

Neural networks are computer systems designed to mimic the path of communication within the human brain. In your body, you have billions of neurons that are all interconnected and travel up through your spine and into your brain. They are attached by root-like nodes that pass messages through each neuron one at a time all the way up the chain until it reaches your brain.

While there is no way to replicate this with a computer yet, we take the principle idea and apply it to computer neural networks to replicate the ability to learn like a human brain learns; recognize patterns and inferring information from the discovery of new information.

In the case of the neural networks, as with all our machine learning models. Information is processed through neural networks as numerical data. By giving out numerical data values, we are giving it the power to use algorithms to make predictions.

Just as with the neurons in the brain, data starts at the top and works its way down, being first separated into nodes. The neural network uses nodes to communicate through each layer. A neural network is comprised of three parts; Input, hidden, and output layers.

In the picture below, we have a visual representation of a neural network, with the circles being every individual node in the network. On the left side, we have the input layer; this is where our data goes in. After the data passes through the input layer, it gets filtered through several hidden layers. The hidden layers are where data gets sorted by different characteristics and features. The hidden layers look for patterns within the data set. The hidden layers are where the 'magic' is happening because the data is being sorted by patterns that we probably wouldn't recognize if we sorted it manually. Each node has a weight which will help to determine the significance of the feature being sorted.

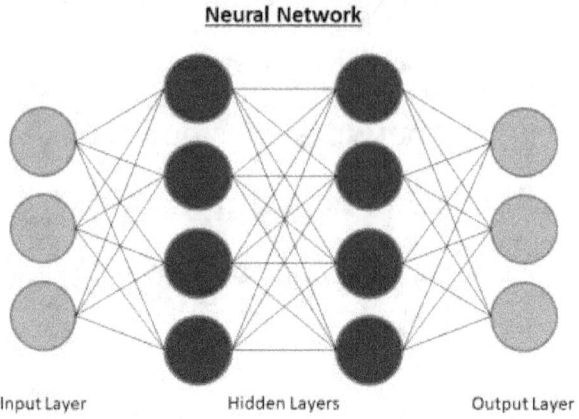

Input Layer   Hidden Layers   Output Layer

The best use of these neural networks would be a task that would be easy for a human but extremely difficult for a computer. Recall at the beginning of the book when we talked about reasoning and inductive reasoning. Our human brain is a powerful tool for inductive reasoning; it's our advantage over advanced computers that can calculate high numbers of data in a matter of seconds. We model neural networks after human thinking because we are attempting to teach a computer how to 'reason' like a human. This is quite a challenge. A good example of a neural network is the example we mentioned we apply neural networks for tasks that would be extremely easy for a human but are very challenging for a computer.

Neural networks can take a huge amount of computing power. The first reason neural networks are a challenge to process is because of the volume of datasets required to make an accurate model. If you want the model to learn how to sort photographs, there are many subtle differences between photos that the model will need to learn to complete the task effectively. That leads to the next challenge, which is the number of variables required for a neural network to work properly. The more data that you use and the higher the number of variables analyzed means that there is an increase in hidden networks. At any given time, several hundred or even thousands of features are being analyzed and classified through the model. Take self-driving cars as an example. Self-driving cars have more than 150 nodes for sorting. This means that the amount of computing power required for a self-driving car to make split-second decisions while analyzing thousands of inputs at a time is quite large.

In the instance of sorting photos, neural networks can be very useful, and the methods that data scientists use are improving rapidly. If I showed you a picture of a dog and a picture of a cat, you could easily tell me which one a cat was, and which one was a dog. But for a computer, this takes sophisticated neural networks and a large volume of data to teach the model.

A common issue with neural networks is overfitting. The model can predict the values for the training data, but when it's exposed to unknown data, it is fit too specifically for the old data and cannot make generalized predictions for new data.

Say that you have a math test coming up and you want to study. You can memorize all the formulas that you think will appear on the test and hope that when the test day comes, you will be able to just plug in the new information into what you've already memorized. Or you can study more deeply; learning how each formula works so that you can produce good results even when the conditions change. An overfitted model is like memorizing the formulas for a test. It will do well if the new data is similar, but when there is a variation, then it won't know how to adapt. You can usually tell if your model is overfitted if it performs well with training data but does poorly with test data.

When we are checking the performance of our model, we can measure it using the cost value. The cost value is the difference between the predicted value and the actual value of our model.

One of the challenges with neural networks is that there is no way to determine the relationship between specific inputs with the output. The hidden layers are called hidden layers for a reason; they are too difficult to interpret or make sense of.

The most simplistic type of neural network is called a perceptron. It's the derives its simplicity from the fact that it has only one layer through which data passes. The input layer leads to one classifying hidden layer, and the resulting prediction is a binary classification. Recall that when we refer to a classification technique as binary, that means it only sorts between two different classes, represented by 0 and 1.

The perceptron was first developed by Frank Rosenblatt. It's a good idea to familiarize yourself with the perceptron if you'd like to learn more about neural networks. The perceptron uses the same process as other neural network models, but typically you'll be working with more layers and more possible outputs. When data is received, the perceptron multiples the input by the weight they are given. Then the sum of all these values is plugged into the activation function. The activation function tells the input which category it falls into, in other words predicting the output.

If you were to look at the perceptron on a graph, its line would appear like this:

$$f(x) = 0 \text{ if } 0 > x, 1 \text{ if } X \geq 0$$

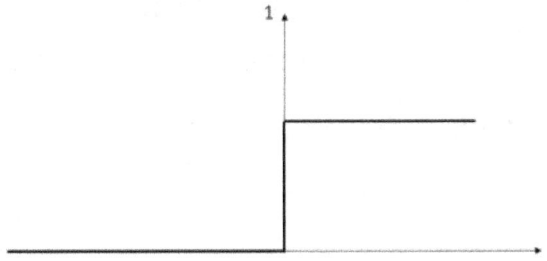

Perceptron Activation Function

The line of the graph of perception appears like a step, with two values, one on either side of the 1. These two sides of the step are the different classes that the model will predict based on the inputs. As you might be able to tell from the graph, it's a bit crude because there is very little separate along the line between classes. Even a small change in some input variable will cause the predicted output to be a different class. It won't perform as well outside of the original dataset that you use for training because it is a step function.

An alternative to the perceptron is a model called a sigmoid neuron. The principle advantage of using the sigmoid neuron is that it is not binary. Unlike perceptron, which can classify data into two categories, the sigmoid function creates a probability rather than a classification. The image below shows the curve of a sigmoid neuron

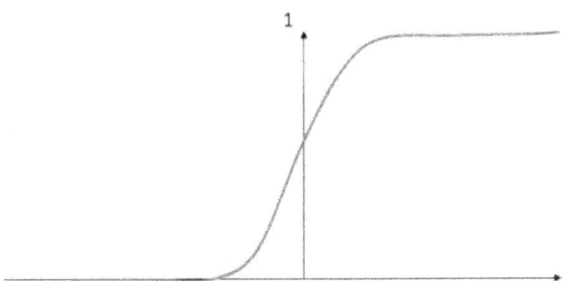

Notice the shape of the curve around one, where the data is sorted with the perceptron; the step makes it difficult to classify data with just marginal differences. With the sigmoid neuron, the data is predicted by the probability that it falls into a given class. As you can see the line curves at one, which means that the probability that a data point falls into a given class increases after one, but it's only a probability.

REINFORCEMENT LEARNING

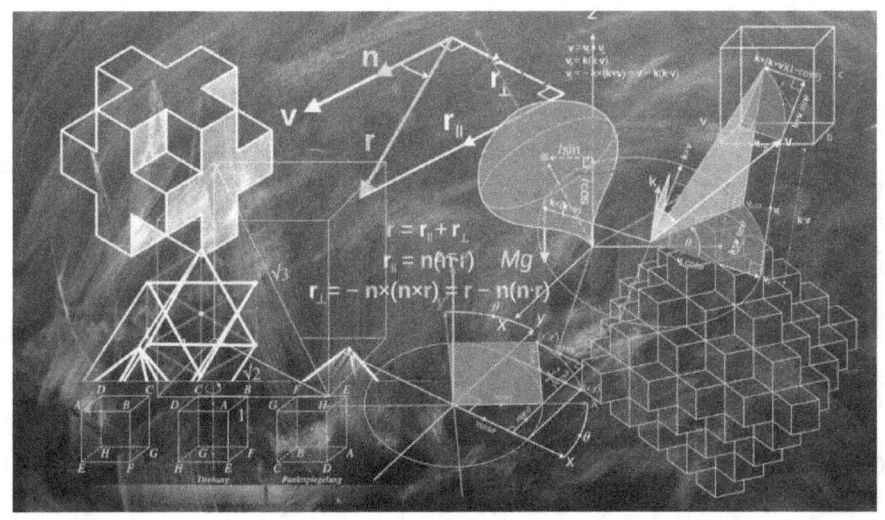

Reinforcement learning is our third kind of machine learning. Like unsupervised learning, no inputs are given. The reinforcement learning model must discover on its own how to be the most effective. Then, the data scientist makes suggests improving the model based on its ability to predict an outcome, which is evaluated by looking at comparisons between prediction and actual value. This is the most progressive type of machine learning, and where much of the machine learning in the future will be done.

Think of it like playing a game; over time, you learn by winning and losing. You learn how to win by playing, and the more you become familiar with the game, the better you understand the mechanics of winning. Over time, the data scientist gives the model feedback as it collects and processes data. It receives a reward signal so that it knows when it is doing a good job of predicting some outcome. So 'winning' the game gives positive feedback to the algorithm. This is the type of machine learning used in gaming, robots, navigation, and self-driving cars.

Q Learning

In Q-learning, the model communicates with its environment to improve itself. You begin by having a set of states. States are the things in the environment which stand as obstacles and avenues in your environment. Called "S." In chess, it would be the way that all of your pieces could move, as well as where all of your opponent's pieces are. These are states.

The possible moves are called 'A.' If you are a pawn, your possible moves are one square forward. If you're a rook, your possible moves are in any direction in a straight line. Q is the value of the model, which starts at 0. As you play the game, Q goes up and down depending on its interactions with the environment. With negative interactions, the score Q goes down. With positive interactions, the score Q goes up. The algorithm learns how to move so that it can optimize the number Q. In the beginning, it's random. Over time, these random movements result in positive and negative effects on Q, and the machine learns how each move will affect the score of Q. It must play a lot of games to improve the way it plays over time. It's much easier said than done to apply this process in real life.

SARSA State Action Reward State Action There is only a small difference between SARSA and Q. They function similarly in giving the model a reward response.

Deep Q network Deep Q is applied when regular Q isn't general enough. When it sees new things that it hasn't seen before, it doesn't know what to do. Q learning can't adjust itself for things it has never seen. Deep Q uses a neural network.

Markov Decision Process Has a Set of possible states, a set of models, a set of possible actions, and a real value reward. This model learns by interacting with the environment through ongoing interaction.

DDPG Deep Deterministic Policy Gradient Another reward state model functions as an actor and a critic.

Semi-Supervised learning

This type of machine learning uses a combination of supervised and unsupervised learning. Some data is labeled while other data is not. But typically, most data will be unlabeled. Semi-supervised learning can be used for classification, regression, and prediction.

Semi-supervised machine learning is helpful because labeling everything would be too time-consuming, and it can harm the ability to find new patterns.

Ensemble Modeling

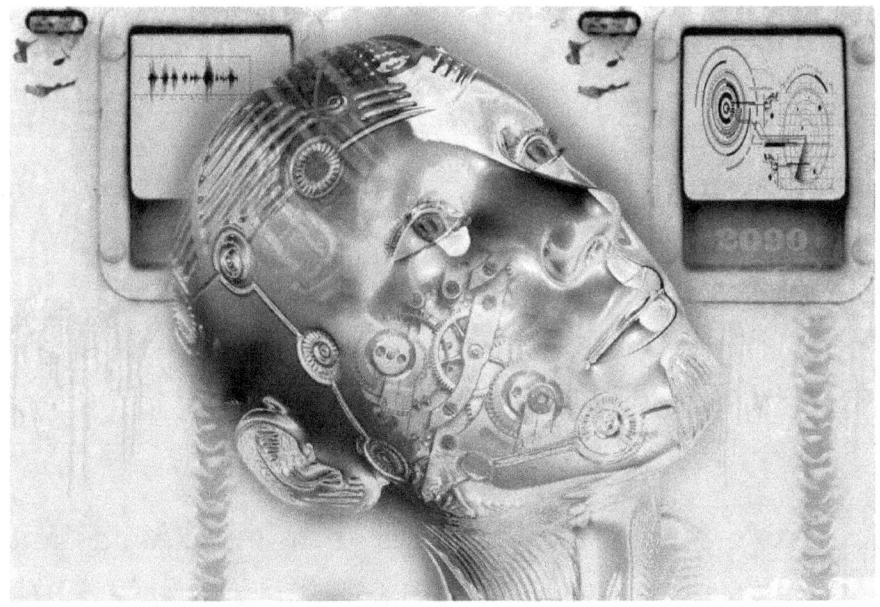

We've learned that diversifying our trees can create a more accurate prediction. But what if, instead of using several versions of the same model, we just used several different models? This is a common trick in machine learning, known as ensemble modeling. By combining information from multiple different types of algorithms, we can improve our model's accuracy and ability to forecast.

Ensemble modeling is all about the divide and conquers mindset. Different models will give us different insights about the data that may not be recognizable by other models. By combining the information attained from different models, we can learn even more about the truth of our data.

Ensemble modeling also helps to minimize bias and variance in our predictions. Individual models may have prediction errors, but the aggregate of all our predictions will be more accurate.

There are a few different methods to use ensemble modeling:

The first is to take the mode of your predictions. That is, take the value which occurs most frequently across the models. Whichever prediction occurs the most frequently, or has the highest number of 'votes,' is the prediction we choose.

We could also take the average of all the predictions, depending on what kind of models we have. The average of all the predictions will be our final prediction. Our ensemble should also consider the reliability of individual models. The results of our models receive different weights, making some predictions more important than others based on reliability.

How do we know which kind of models we want to combine? We already know from this book that there are several types of models to choose from, each giving us different possibilities and advantages.

A common pair of models is using neural networks and decision trees together. Neural networks give us new information, and the decision tree ensures that we have not missed anything.

In addition to the bootstrapping and bagging that we discussed earlier, there are a few other ways of doing ensemble modeling. Data scientists use what's called a bucket of models. Here they use several different types of models to use with the test data and then choose the one that did the best.

Another idea is called stacking. Stacking uses several different types of models and then uses all the results to give us a prediction that is a combination of all of them.

Data scientists like to use ensemble modeling because, with a variety of models, we can usually produce better predictions than with a single model alone.

The drawback to ensemble modeling is that we lose some of our readability. Having multiple models working together at once makes interpretation more difficult, especially when you want to share the data with stakeholders who don't have data science knowledge.

We can also use several versions of the same model, like how random forests improve the forecast with multiple versions of itself — using neural networks with different sets of nodes and different values for k, or numbers of clusters to see how that changes the outcome of our prediction and find if there is an optimal value for k, or if there are groups or subgroups that we may have overlooked.

It doesn't do as much when we already have a strong model. But if we combine a few models that have weaker forecasting abilities, then it usually improves the overall accuracy.

THINGS YOU MUST KNOW FOR MACHINE LEARNING

To be successful with machine learning, you must have the right tools in order to work, just like if you were building a house, you would need to skills and the tools required. The following is a list of the required materials to do machine learning.

Data

To start working with your data, you have to have enough data to break it into two categories; training data and test data.

Training data is the data you use in the beginning when you are building your model. When you are first creating your model, you need to give it some data to learn from. With training data, you will already know the independent variables as well as their respective dependent variables. This means that for every input, you will already know the output of your data. From this data, your model will learn to predict the output on its own. Our training data gives us the parameters we need to make predictions. This is the data that our machine learns from.

Test data is the data that the machine gets once you are satisfied with the model, and you see what it does out in the wild. In this data, we only have the independent variables, but no output. With test data, we can see how well our model does at predicting an outcome with new data.

Your training data should account for most of your data; approximately 70%, while your test data is the remaining 30%. In order to avoid bias, make sure that the data you choose for training data and test data is totally random when you split them up. Don't choose which data to use; let it be random. Don't use the same data for training and testing. Start by giving the training data to the machine and examine the relationships between X and Y, then try to see how well your model did.

The most important question to consider during this process is whether your model will still work when it is presented with new data. You can test this by doing cross-validation. This means you will test your model on data you have not used yet. Keep some data to the side that you didn't use during training to see how accurate your model is at the end.

You can also use K-fold validation to check the accuracy of your model. This method is pretty easy to use and generally unbiased. It's a good technique to use when we don't have a lot of data to work with for testing. For K-fold validation, we will break our data into k folds, usually between 5 and 10. Test each fold and see how they performed across all the folds once you are finished with testing. Usually, the larger your number for k is the less biased your test will be.

So far, we have talked about models interpreting data to find meaning and patterns. But what kind of data are we going to use? Where will we get our data, and what is it going to look like?

Data is the most critical component for machine learning. After all, your model will only learn with data, so it's important that you have data that is relevant and meaningful. It came come in many shapes and sizes, structure differently depending on the kinds of data. The more structured the data is, the easier it is to work with. Some data has very little structure, and this data is harder to interpret. Data for facial recognition can be huge and have very little meaning to the untrained eye.

Structured data is more organized. This is the type of data that you will likely use when you are first starting out. It will help you get your feet wet, and you can start understanding the statistic involved in machine learning. Usually, structure data will come in a familiar form that looks something like this, in rows and columns. This is called a tabular dataset.

Market Value	num_bedrooms	num_bathrooms	Sq_ft	pool (Y/N)
$207,367	4	3	2635	N
$148,224	3	2	1800	Y
$226,897	5	3.5	2844	Y
$122,265	2	1.5	1644	N

Recall that a feature is some measurable characteristic of a variable. In each column in a tabular dataset, we see a feature. This feature is some measurable dimension or attribute. Here we have used data reflecting the market value of a house as a function of the number of bedrooms, the number of bathrooms, square footage, and whether the house has a pool. Our market value is the Y; this is our dependent variable. Our independent variables, or our Xs, are num_bedrooms, num_bathrooms, st_ft, and pool.

In supervised learning, you will already have the Y in your dataset. In this case, it's the market value of the home. With enough of this data in our model, even if we don't know the market value of a house we should be able to predict it if we have the number of bedrooms, the number of bathrooms, square footage, and whether the house has a pool or not. Data that is organized in this way is relatively easy to work with and have multiple independent variables like this makes this an example of the multivariate regression.

How much data should you use?

There is no set rule to how much data you will need for your model, but there are guidelines which you should follow. The most important thing is that when you have several independent variables to analyze, then your model will work the best if your data has as many possible combinations of the independent variables as you can get. If you do this, your model will still work even when it encounters a new combination of features that it hasn't seen before. It will have a pretty good way of predicting, even if the combination is completely new.

A good general rule to follow is that you should have about ten times as many respondents as we do independent variables. In the case of our market value example above, we have num_bedrooms, num_bathrooms, sq_ft, and pool. This is four different independent variables, which means we should have at least forty respondents like the ones listed above to create a reliable model.

Having a lot of variables can help us predict the Y more accurately, but that that be costly and make your data harder to process. You must also consider how you are pooling your data. The market values of houses in Los Angeles will be much different than the market values of houses in Cleveland.

It's also important to keep features as relevant as possible. Having multiple variables will help you make a better prediction, but there are variables that may just create bias in the model.

Refer to Scikit learn to see what they recommend for data sizes for certain types of analysis.

But not all data is useful. We often talk about big data, and it might be easy to assume that the more data we have, the better. But that's not always the case. Some data may not be helpful. Certain variables might get in the way and may make it harder to find the true answer.

Preparing the Data

So now you have your data, but how do you get it to a point where it's readable by your model? Data will rarely suit our modeling needs right out of the gate. For our data to be formatted properly, it usually requires a round of data cleaning first. The process of data cleaning is often referred to as data scrubbing.

We might have data that comes in the form of images or emails. We need to rewrite it so that it has numerical values that will be interpretable by our algorithms. After all, our machine learning models are algorithms or math equations, so the data needs to have numerical values for it to be modeled.

You might also have pieces of data that were recorded incorrectly or in the wrong format. There may be variables that you don't need, and you must get rid of. It can be tedious and time-consuming but its extremely important to have data that will work and can easily be read by your model. It's the least sexy part of being a data scientist.

This is the part of machine learning where you will probably spend most of your time. As a data scientist, you will probably spend about 20% of your time doing data science and the other 80% of your time making sure your data is clean and ready to be processed by your model. We may be combining multiple types of data, and we need to reformat the recordings so that they fit together. First, in the case of supervised learning, pick the variables that you think are most important for your model. If we choose irrelevant variables or variables that don't matter, we may create a bias and could make our model less effective.

A simple example of cleaning or scrubbing data is recoding a response for gender. On your data, you have a column for male/female. Unfortunately, male and female do not have a numerical value. But you can easily change this by making this a binary variable. Assign female = 1 and male =0. Now you can find a numerical value for the effect that being a female has on the outcome of your model.

We can also combine variables to make it simpler to interpret. Let's say you are creating a regression model that predicts a person's income based on several variables. One of the variables is the education level, which you have recorded in years. So, the possible responses for years of education are 1, 2, 3, 4, 5, 6, 7, 8, 9, 10, 11, 12, 13, 14, 15, 16. This is a lot of discrete categories. You could simplify it by creating groups. For example, you could rewrite variables 1, 2, 3, 4, 5, 6, 7, 8 = primary_ed and rewrite 9, 10, 11, 12 = secondary_ed and rewrite 13, 14, 15, 16 = tertiary education. Instead of having twelve categories, you have three. Respondents either have some primary education, secondary education, or some level of post-secondary or college-level education. This is known as binning data, and it can be a good way to clean up your data if it's used properly.

When you are combining variables to make interpretation simpler, you must consider the tradeoff between having more streamlined data and losing some important information about relationships in the data. Consider that in this example, by combining these variables into three groups instead of sixteen, you may be creating bias in your model.

There a lot of factors that could require you to clean your data. Even a misspelling or an extra space somewhere in your data can have a negative impact on your model.

You might have data that is missing. In order to fix this situation, you can replace the missing values with either the mode of the median of that variable. It's possible to remove data with missing values if there are only a few, but this just means you'll have fewer data to use in your model.

Programming Tools

In order to process your data, you will need special programming tools so you can tell the data what you want it to do. We have already mentioned that machine learning is a branch of computer science. This is where that comes into play.

In the introduction, we said that the three most common languages for data science are Python, R, and C++. Choosing which one is right for you will depend on your experience and what you are planning to do with your data.

The most common language for data science is python. It was created in 1991 by Guido Van Rossum, and it's notable because it is easier to read than other programming languages. It's still being developed and improved today. It's not complicated to learn and is compatible with most relevant data types. It also has applications outside of mere data manipulation that will be useful in machine learning.

Python has several free packages that you can install which have been created to give you shortcuts to common data science tools. These packages have shortcuts for codes that are commonly used in machine learning, which makes you must do less of the work.

Pandas is a must-have library of tools for data scientists working with python. It allows you to manipulate time-series data and tabular datasets more easily. It shows your data in rows and columns so that it's easier to manage, in much the same way that you would look at data in Microsoft excel. It's easy to find online and free to download. Pandas is helpful when you're looking at datasets in .CSV format.

Numpy is a helpful program to do data processing faster using python. It works similarly to Matlab, and it can handle matrices and multi-dimensional data. It will help you import large datasets easier.

Scikit-learn is another library of the machine learning function. With Scikit learn, you will have easy access to many of the algorithms that we have mentioned earlier, which are commonly used in machine learning. Algorithms like classification, regression, clustering, support vector, random forest, and k-means have shortcuts so that a lot of the grunt coding is done for you.

R is the third option. It's free to use and open source. R can be used for both data mining and machine learning. It's popular for those who are new to data science because of its availability. It can't handle the larger datasets required for more advanced machine learning operations, but it's not a bad place to start if you are new to data science and computer programming.

In order to run these programs, you will need a computer. Usually, a regular laptop or desktop computer will be powerful enough to process smaller and medium-sized datasets, especially when you are new to machine learning.

Although GPUs (Graphics Processing Units) have existed for some time, their accessibility has increased in recent years, which makes data science more accessible. It has been a breakthrough in the field of data science because the field is no longer limited to labs with massive computers.

GPUs are known for being the power behind video games. They allow a computer to interpret multiple points at once, which is essential for processing volumes of data. Now GPUs allow us to do a lot more with much less computer hardware. The predecessor, CPU cores head multiple control units that allowed information to be processed all at once. Rather than having multiple control units, the GPU has a much larger web of cores that can all handle different processes all at once. One GPU card can contain almost 5000 processors. It's a major advancement for artificial intelligence and machine learning. They can help make the processing of neural networks much faster.

C and C++ are other common data analysis languages. The advantage of C++ is that it is a very powerful language. It can process massive data sets very quickly. Data scientists using massive datasets often choose to use C++ for its speed and processing power, especially when working with datasets over a terabyte. C++ can process one gigabyte of data in about a second. This makes it especially useful for deep learning algorithms, neural network models with 5-10 layers, and huge datasets. This type of model might be overwhelming for software that isn't as fast. If you are doing more advanced machine learning and you have multiple GPUs, then C++ might be the language for you. C++ is capable of just about anything; it's a very versatile language.

The downside is that the libraries in C++ aren't as extensive as those in Python. This means that when you are writing code for your data and model, you'll likely be starting from scratch. No matter what kind of projects you decide to do, there will be roadblocks as you write your code. Having a library that can help you when you get stuck will enable you to learn and work faster.

Developing Models

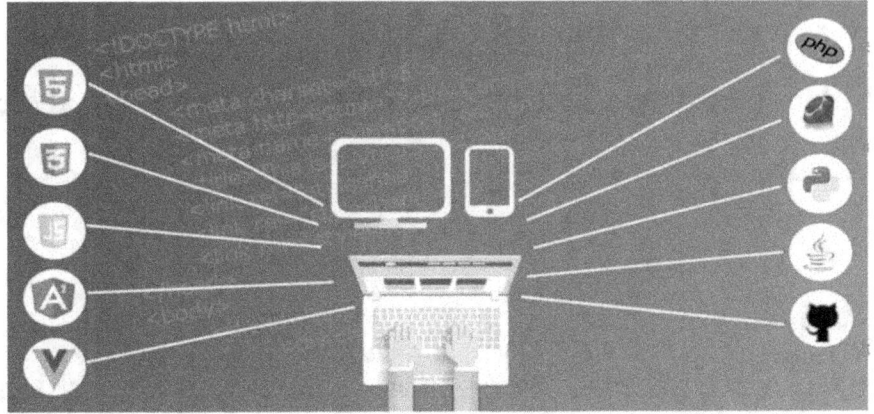

You will need to get yourself set up in Python or some other programming language to do machine learning. You create machine learning models by using code to manipulate the datasets. While this book doesn't cover coding for machine learning, I will give you a quick rundown of some basic libraries and packages that I recommend you install for machine learning.

Because it's the most common language used in data science, we will use Python as an example throughout this chapter. I also think it's the most practical language to learn if it's your first language because it's more readable than other programming languages, and it has a wide range of abilities beyond machine learning.

Once you've installed the latest version of Python, there are a few recommended libraries to install which come with a lot of commands that will be useful to your work with machine learning. All of these can be found easily with a quick google search, and they can be downloaded for free.

The most important library for data analysis and machine learning in Python is called Pandas. It's quite a popular choice for datasets and will make your coding easier and faster, especially when you are still trying to get a feel for things.

Anaconda for python

Another option for getting yourself started with Python is installing Anaconda. The great thing about Anaconda is that it gives you every package for Python so that you don't have to install packages one at a time while you write the program for your model. It comes with all the libraries you will need, for just about every different kind of function.

Anaconda is a free and open-source program that will work in both R and Python. With Anaconda, you'll have access to several libraries that will help you with your data science projects. Basically, this gives you a pre-packaged collection of all the python libraries, of which there are over 100 libraries.

One of the major libraries is Spyder and Jupyter. Both of these are integrated development environments, meaning they are the window where you will write your code, but they are more developed than a standard command window and have options to save and export/import codes.

Most Python users will start in a development environment called IDLE. It's very simple and offers a good format for learning how to code in python. When you install Python on a windows computer, it will come automatically included. If you have a Linux computer, it is available, but you will need to install it separately.

IDLE will make those baby steps in Python easier because you'll be able to save your scripts and edit them later. It will also walk you through debugging.

To install Anaconda, visit:

docs.anaconda.com/anaconda/install

Scroll down until you see a list of operating systems. Choose your operating system. It will give you instructions for installing anaconda on their website, based on your operating system. Then you're ready to start messing around in Python. I highly recommend using one of the free beginner Python tutorials that are available on the internet. EdX has a free beginner tutorial in Python, which is a great place to start. Also, take advantage of forums like Reddit, where there have been a vast number of common questions already answered in detail, and members are always sharing relevant news from the world of machine learning.

Algorithms

Once you have your data, and the hardware and software to manipulate it, you need to bring them together. Put your data on your programming software. Find a dataset for free online to work with when you are first starting out. Kaggle.com is free and has a lot of data sets to choose from in CSV format, which will be easy to work with once you have Pandas library imported into your Python.

The best algorithms to start with are linear and logistic regression for supervised learning and k-means clusters in unsupervised learning. These will be relatively easy starting out, and you can build towards other models from there.

Visualization tools

You have your data, and now you have created models using one of the programming languages, and you have a whole collection of data science libraries to help you do all this faster. Your computer is running well, and you can create models independently.

You may have created models that display interesting results, but in order to break it down into layman's terms and communicate your findings with stakeholders, you'll need to organize it in a way that's easy to visualize. If you're a data scientist on a marketing project, you may have created a model that helps break down customers into categories and predicts trends in buying habits. But if you want to communicate these results to the rest of your marketing team, you'll need to find a way to communicate so that even people who aren't familiar with data science can understand your results. Breaking down your data into charts and graphs and visual will help compliment your analytics skills. Being able to make visualizations of your data is extremely important when you are communicating with an audience who isn't familiar with data analysis

A popular toolset for data professionals is Tableau. Tools like these are called data visualization software. At some companies, there are employees whose entire job involves taking hard to read data and presenting it in a way that is easy to visualize.

Software like tableau is very commonly used by businesses that rely on data to make decisions. Tableau is useful because its relatively easy to use, and data can be viewed in real-time through its platform. You can customize a dashboard of tools for creating reports and charts with your data. It also gives you the ability to share your results with other people from your company. Tableau can be used to create graphs and scatterplots from that data that you have analyzed in your programming language.

More advanced things which are useful

These tools may not be as relevant to you when you are just beginning, but it might be interesting to talk about some of them and consider what may be useful down the road. This book may just the beginning on your path to be a machine learning expert, so you may refer to this list later when you are a little more advanced.

You should continue to think about the management of unstructured data. Usually, this requires more advanced programs because it is more difficult to manage and manipulate. This type of data often takes on the form of something much too complicated for the human brain to analyze without the assistance of tools, but this is the direction where machine learning is heading. Using neural networks to mimic the functions of human thought, who knows what the future will hold.

The further we get with machine learning, the bigger our data is getting. Possibilities of machine learning are expanding all the time. The data that is important in the future won't have the neat structure we are accustomed to, like the kind of data that can fit in an excel sheet.

This type of data also requires beefier computer hardware and software to be able to handle the processing of these large quantities of information. Usually use some sort of cloud computing software to carry the large volumes of information, as well as a GPU specific to data analytics. This higher level of computing can help to process multiple moving points at once. The math required also becomes harder. Combining algorithms.

AFTERWORD

Hopefully, after reading this book, you have a good understanding of the basic principles of machine learning. You've now been introduced to several different types of popular machine learning models and their uses. We've explored how advanced data scientists are using machine learning to create predictions and the parameters that they need to create predictions that are accurate and dependable when introduced to new data.

The beauty of data science and machine learning is the broad range of applications. If you go out and gain machine learning experience, then there is a broad range of jobs and opportunities working with all different kinds of data. Whether you like the competition and the rush of business, and you want to use models that predict the rise and fall in stocks or guess what a customer will buy next. Or maybe you have an interest in medicine and health care; you can apply machine learning to improve cancer diagnosis and get new insight into the characteristics of a disease and how it will affect different individuals. Wherever your interests may lie, there is an opportunity for machine learning to be implanted to improve upon what we can already do.

The more that the world becomes connected, the more data will become available. Almost everyone has some type of smart device recording and tracking of their user data. Data scientists are finding more creative ways to learn from and interpret that data. Machine learning is a way for data scientists to examine trends that are beyond the scope of human comprehension, which means that our predictions will continue to get more accurate and our data more useful.

Computers will only continue to get more powerful, and that power will become more and more accessible which means that machine learning and data science will no longer be just buzzwords but widely applied methods of finding valuable information. It's not just large businesses utilizing data and machine learning anymore; it's becoming more feasible for even smaller businesses to incorporate big data into their decision-making processes.

Now that you know the basic theory of machine learning, its time for you to keep going and find ways to apply and practice the knowledge. If you are interested in being a data scientist that specializes in machine learning, this book is only the beginning of the process. I highly recommend you commit yourself to learn a language like Python, R, or C++. It's the next step in becoming a data scientist, and in applying these machine learning theories into actual models and algorithms. Thanks to the internet, there is a vast number of books, videos, and tutorials available for free that will take you through the process of learning computer languages. There has never been a better time to learn how to code and create your own models. This book is only a small piece of a large collection of information available on the subject. If you're serious about machine learning, then this shouldn't be the only book you read.

You can find entire books describing the process of specific models. Neural networks are a field that is so advanced that you could find entire books based on that specific type of model alone. It's not a bad idea to pick up a few statistics study guides so that you can refer to them when you have a question. Be on the lookout for possible sources of data that you might be able to utilize, and potential questions that may be interesting to explore with statistical mathematics.

The job opportunities alone are enough reason to pursue further knowledge in the field. There is a shortage of experienced data scientists who can apply the methods and techniques listed in this book. This means there is an opportunity for someone who wills to get their hands dirty and start coding their own models. There are businesses and organizations out there, right now, searching for people who can use this information properly. Keep in mind that this demand won't exist forever. Already, universities across the globe are creating new degree programs specifically geared towards data science as a blend of computer science and statistics. This means that the next generation of data scientists is already on their way.

So, begin your learning now. Find an online tutorial and some free datasets online and start figuring out how to regress and classify, using this book as a guide. Learn each model one at a time. Find examples on the internet of finished models and try to see if you can replicate the results. It takes time to learn programming languages, so be patient and seek out new opportunities to learn and adapt your skills.

Try one of the online communities specific to statistical modeling in order to cut your teeth and learn from what other data scientists are doing. I advise you to check out Kaggle.com. It's a website that hosts statistical modeling competition for aspiring data scientists. Different companies and organizations post contests with the datasets included. It's a great way to experiment with a variety of tasks and get data to work with. Old contests are also available online, with a large number of associated tutorials on youtube.com and other data science communities for you to learn from. It's probably the best way for an aspiring data scientist to expand his/her resume and network with other data scientists.

If you found this useful you could also like:

PYTHON MACHINE LEARNING

Discover the Essentials of Machine Learning, Data Analysis, Data Science, Data Mining and Artificial Intelligence Using Python Code with Python Tricks

By Samuel Hack

I would like to thank you for reading this book and if you enjoyed it I would appreciate your review on Amazon!

www.ingramcontent.com/pod-product-compliance
Lightning Source LLC
Chambersburg PA
CBHW070626220526
45466CB00001B/103